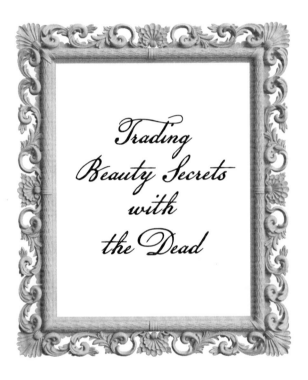

Trading
Beauty Secrets
with
the Dead

ALSO BY ERINA HARRIS

The Stag Head Spoke

Trading

BEAUTY
SECRETS

with the Dead

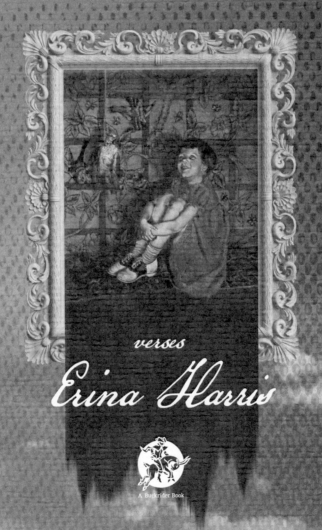

verses

Erina Harris

A Buckrider Book

Selima Hill, "The Dolls," *Splash Like Jesus* (Bloodaxe Books, 2017). Reprinted with permission of the publisher. www.bloodaxebooks.com

Published by Buckrider Books
an imprint of Wolsak and Wynn Publishers
280 James Street North
Hamilton, ON L8R2L3
www.wolsakandwynn.ca

Editor: Paul Vermeersch | Copy editor: Ashley Hisson
Cover and interior design: Kilby Smith-McGregor
Cover image painting: *In the Dark* by Dana Holst
Author photograph: Evan Will
Typeset in FreightText Pro, American Scribe and B eastly
Printed by Coach House Printing Company, Toronto, Canada

10 9 8 7 6 5 4 3 2 1

The publisher gratefully acknowledges the support of the Canada Council for the Arts and the Ontario Arts Council. We also acknowledge the financial support of the Government of Canada through the Canada Book Fund and the Government of Ontario through the Ontario Book Publishing Tax Credit and Ontario Creates.

Library and Archives Canada Cataloguing in Publication
Title: Trading beauty secrets with the dead : verses / Erina Harris.
Names: Harris, Erina, author.
Identifiers: Canadiana 20240427459 | ISBN 9781998408030 (softcover)
Subjects: LCGFT: Poetry.
Classification: LCC PS8615.A74783 T73 2024 | DDC C811/.6—dc23

For Anne, mother.

For Rob, brother.

For Mary Jo Bang, fairy godmother.

And for the Rhyming Women.

The invention of printing coincided with the invention of childhood.

Susan Stewart, *On Longing*

In effect, to understand correctly
The term, rhyme – what other is there besides
Full of new rhymes – Death?
For no exit: language is worn out.

Marina Tsvetaeva, "Letter from the New Year"
to Rainer Maria Rilke (Trans. Gabriella Bedetti)

And nonsense more nonsense is sullen.

Gertrude Stein, *Tender Buttons*

✦✦ **Dramatis Personae,** *The Letters* ✦✦

Letter A:
A Grammar, And, An Ekphrasis
Waiting Room, Part I: Letter A *to* Letter B

In truth, Jacob far preferred the company of Aunt Schlemmer, his father's widowed sister, to that of his own mother. Every day, he and Wilhelm would walk to her house, where they spent more time than in the Grimm home. Juliane Schlemmer was worldly and learned, a childless widow. Because she was supported by her brother Philipp, she had ample time ... to teach her young nephews their ABCs.

VALERIE PARADIŽ, *Clever Maids: The Secret History of the Grimm Fairy Tales*

On stilts, still, Letter A awaits,
crossing its arms

across itself: Two brooms in a room
atop a shelf meet, in A, and wait,

awaiting room. In a Waiting Room
an A is first, staring in a room

inside itself. Within, it must open,
and without, A must, every bit more

and less itself stand up straight,
uncrossing from its midriff, open – (

and almost stop;
As elephantine otherness rushes in

and stays) – then wrap at tip and toe
each arm around,

to come to be Two rooms within and
out (Her forehead pressed

alongside her forehead) so
Letter B can be beside its self.

Letter B:
Bestiary Rondo

"No, dear Beast," answered Beauty, softly.

<small>MADAME DE VILLENEUVE,</small> *Beauty and the Beast* (1740)

...

... in the breath, in the breeze, that the breathing beasts breathe in, the breaths of the bees breathing trees' breaths, the breeze breathes the bee-breaths with trees breathing beast-breaths, breath breezes in beast-breathing bees breathe the bee-breathing trees in the breath-tree will be in the breeze of the bee in the tree-bees will breathe with breeze-breaths will beasts bleed ... [*Da Capo*]

Letter C:
"'Chloe liked Olivia.' by Mary Carmichael
and, or, Virginia Woolf"

First she broke the sentence; now she has broken the sequence.
  VIRGINIA WOOLF, *A Room of One's Own*

...

Without meaning to, inevitably lie. In imagination, I had gone into. A laboratory.
(He pointed out to women that dark place at the back of the head. Our own sex
was unable.) A pen in her. Receptacle. Drawing room or nursery. First she broke.

Between. The Violet sellers. And crones. Her alternations. Or a pickaxe.
(Women, are too simple.) A more fitting. Neither. May be beginning. I
had gone. In imagination. (Something. Harlots or courtesans.) A labour.

Neither. More fitting receptacle. She went over it like a bird.
At the end of a shelf. So respectable. Booted and furred. (That she believes it.)
Indelibly. In cupboards. And other distinctions. First she broke

the sentence. A prison yard. The English language. Goes into a room. The rooms
differ. Thunderous. Contrary. Might mean that she was. I was almost sure. (I am
sorry to break.) Inevitably. In imagination, I had gone into. A laboratory. Of

relation. Or from drifting girls. And a fence beyond that. Or. Caves where one
goes with. (Perhaps, the play, required no more.) She (innumerably ancient)
broke the sentence. What happens. Clapping and crying. Money on her back.

Not for the sake. Of breaking. Without doing anything violent I can show
the meaning of all this. (The smooth gliding interrupted.) To the shelves which
hold. Imagine. I had. A laboratory. Her hand. Broke the sentence.
Were invented. Greatly if we insisted. (How.) Chloe watched.

Letter D:
Debtor's Cabaret, Libretto for the Puppet Show

Les Demimondaines, Poem I

Demi-monde: "half-world" (French, 1850s onwards)

Within the half-world, "les demimondaines" were a special breed of enterprising entertainers – bon vivants, frequently courtesans – considered both déclassée and subversive, and immersed within underground societies resplendent with nightlife, art, fashion, sexualities, eclecticisms and versions of relations.

THE MACABRE SILHOUETTE: Nevertheless, the Parlour was inconsolable.

THE PARLOUR: *There's no place like home.*

THE CEILING: Come the Salt, come the Pepper!
... Let down your hair!

CHANDELIER IN THE SHAPE
OF AN EYEGLASS: *Come the Slut! Come the Pauper!*
I have something in my eye ... *You there!*

THE CHECKERBOARD FLOOR
(To the Corner): My Elbow!

THE SILK WALLPAPER
(To the Doorknob): *My Knee.*

TRAIL OF BREADCRUMBS: I just wanted to say ... that the Glancing
Door owes Everything to the Wall.

THE WALL
(To the Glancing Door):   I help you with your being tall.

THE LOVERS: *Despite everything –*

ROCKING HORSE: "There must be more money."

THE LOVERS: *– we were a banquet!*

THE INCITING INCIDENT: *And yet.*

EUGÈNE IONESCO (To the
Inciting Incident):   Beware *Pig-Headed Child*: of the Girl who lives –

MEANWHILE: – meanwhile, back in the fork drawer.

SOMETHING BORROWED: The mob of Sugar Tongs and Custard Cups has
yet to rise up.

THE PARLOUR: *Then, Nightfall.*

Letter E:
The Education of Little Miss Muffet

After Father died, I had all the wrong thoughts.
Stepfather, a Man of Science, prescribes Spiders:
For My Condition. Both Common, and Endangered,

crumpled onto teatime curds, or confined within
sentient globules of butter. One writhes in a nutshell,
when threaded at the neck. *For Fever, or Ungovernable Emotion.*

On occasion, they forget their lines. Some erupt
from labelled bottles he keeps all over the house. Stepfather,
Perturbed by my bouts of shrieking (How he creeps

in my chamber at night. Those hairy legs. Tufted!
I can't stand the sight) then it's *Off! to the Hysterium!*
Little Miss, must rest. Where he takes away my journals

(and then nothing happens but the silk wallpaper),
leaves me only his hornbook made of gingerbread
with Arachnids, discreetly beaten into the batter.

It was the most concentrated moment of my life.
I listen with my ankles in case Father is watching.
In my abdomen I make thoughts trace diaphanous lines

silken striping diagonal all the way to the sill
of the high turret window. What *patience!*
when climbing one two seven ten eleven, then down

the sticky rungs of the lattice sometimes the room
tilts getting mixed in with the pudding (feminine foot-
steps in the hall could belong to anyone) I am spinning.

Letter F:
Folktale

I

Today the Supervisor saw her finished.
He nodded, spat.   Today, she was perfected.

They wrap her up in a red plastic tarp.

                    Tomorrow, they will unveil her.

In that moment your neighbour's sunburnt daughter will look up from her
picture book.

II

For days workers climbed up and down ladders.
                                            Crossing the beam
To press out creases about her lips and cheeks.
                        Some sung rock songs as they worked tall brooms

Dipped in pails of hot paste. Hammers rung nails.
The people of the town came to look.

They smoke thoughtfully.
And imagine her names,
                        Nurse them in her shade.

The dunce-girl kicked out of class purses her lips over gap teeth,
And watches from the courtyard,

        "Everything I did,
        She saw everything."

III

To stand in semidarkness.
Six little girls and one boy hold vigil, self-lit in petticoats that blow and tease.

Flicker, flicker at her feet.

"Tomorrow they'll unveil that big lady. Let's wait."

After a while they, shivering, reluctant, trundle off.

"No.
Let's go."

IV

Later, two merry vandals show.
One is counting stars.
The other sprays graffiti on the sheet that covers her.
A blotch where her crotch would be. *Hi ho.*

Then both depart.

V

Many nights the man climbed to the top of his building, reached the ledge
without rails.

At the woman.

Her look pulls. And silence he cannot explain to his mother.
There is the moon.

Tonight he will go up close.

He mounts the rusty ladder,
Rips tape from the tarp that covers her. Unstartled,

She sits with legs outstretched across the billboard. Up close, her large eyes filled
with dots,

Her look

        At his far, emptied rooftop station.

He pulls a flap, tears off a strip, and places his hand at her missing shoulder.

A dog barks, no sound.

Letter G:
The Gift

After Elizabeth Bishop, "Visits to St. Elizabeths"

Rhyme is an ethic.
        HENRI MESCHONNIC, "Rhyme and Life," Trans. Gabriella Bedetti

...

Bewildered, the children called for "some rhymes."

Come, meet the Inventor!
in the Time of Rhyme.

To invent Ends of Endings,
the Inventrix attempts
to rewind the Rhyme, so

She greets the Clock Doctor who expresses blue shock
at Her Task-Never-Ending, and who never whines
to the Inventrix, however tempting,
to chime by the Slag heap, all the while, Rhyming-

Women arrive
at Seven O'Clock
through the Door at the End
of the Grandmother Clock whose crimes invent
mendings, and thread wooden gums, ever rendering the Brine of Rime

Through the Paper Door, "Enter!":
Blue Women who polish Grandmother
Clock's face and her river-veined hands,
with Brushes Threaded with End-Rhymes {and Eyelashes
of Henchmen}; sidestepping convention,
without condescension, out of line in the Primer of Rime,

Backward-Facing Hearses. The Language Nurses
arrive in order, descending: "To Adore Her, and –
forwards!" with the Before-Women they feather and pluck
from her dusty Clock-Petals her renditions, pendulous –
collect them, intending, to endow them,
and sending, and penned, and endless – "To the Inventory" – past
the thrashing Clothesline of Unrhyme.

Through the Wound in the Rhyme
the Nurses rehearse, sanding her wooden scrolls
{"She was reaching for words through the back of the door –"}
when Daughters ascend the runs in her stockings,
tend her ticking Escapements, her Pendulum, "Rest –"
her swollen archives in that sapphire Compendium.
Their ventriloquy, timeless, "To defend the Impending" {The Hammers
the Pulleys, the Weights that await} and pending, in time, with the Rhymes.

Letter H:
Halfpenny Opera – *The Adventures of Two Pincushion Dolls*

Les Demimondaines, Poem II

In other words, people form their opinion of a young lady from her personal appearance; and if, because she is at work, and in want of pins, and destitute of a Pincushion, she has quite undressed herself, and her clothes are dropping off, she will be thought a negligent slattern.

MARY ANN KILNER,
The Adventures of a Pincushion: Designed Chiefly for the Use of Young Ladies

At length, the Queen interfered: "Let her alone; – who's she? It's my birthday, and we'll play Hunt the Pincushion."

... So Hunt the Pincushion it was. This game is simple and demands only a moderate amount of skill ...

The Pincushion was poor little Flora. How she strained and ducked and swerved to this side or that, in the vain effort to escape her tormentors! Quills with every quill erect tilted against her.

CHRISTINA ROSSETTI,
Speaking Likenesses

Because it was sullied by neglect, not circulation, the pincushion stands for a lonely spinster who is redeemable, rather than a prostitute whose life cannot be salvaged.

BONNIE BLACKWELL,
"Corkscrews and Courtesans: Sex and Death in Circulation Novels"

I

CHLOE: I want to be the Narrator.
OLIVIA: You are *always* the Narrator.

OLIVIA: When I am twenty, I will buy some arms.
CHLOE: They will suit you.
OLIVIA: I could get some porcelain hands, too. Like you.

II

"I would welcome respite from the Lady's Chamber,"
Chloe said.

"All they do is talk about That Gentleman's Money!"
replied Olivia.

"Or Kissy Kissy," said I, clacking my eyes.
"Or the worst – Kissy Kissy *and* Money!" said Olivia.

"And never about The Big Thing!"
"And then."

"Then the lights go out. The singing."
"Then it's all just ..."

III

CHLOE: Up here, where.

OLIVIA: And then time goes different.

CHLOE:	You traipsing on tippytoe; I dragging my arms –
OLIVIA:	and her scissors shrieking molten tassels.

CHLOE:	And then: *to swoon!*

OLIVIA:	To faint from a great height ...
CHLOE:	into a giant pile of wool
OLIVIA:	emits a torrent of spores, fibres
CHLOE:	delirious and filaments first-born snowflakes,

OLIVIA:	*when the Big Poof!*

IV

"I am so pleased," Chloe said. "And ..."

"*Again –*" gasped Chloe and Olivia in near-unison.

V. Chloe and Olivia Spend an Afternoon in the Room Filled with Confections

CHLOE:	What preening pastries!
OLIVIA:	(*Whispering*) Those Cakes are kind of stupid.

CHLOE:	What quivering custards!
OLIVIA:	To curdle in the thicket.
CHLOE:	Her cinnamon turret!
CHLOE:	A crumpet,
OLIVIA:	a strumpet.

CHLOE:	Pucker-pucker, the ruffle-tufts!
OLIVIA:	*Preposterous.*

CHLOE:	What curt spurt of treacle,
OLIVIA:	what cruel almandine muff.
CHLOE:	Engirdled, portentous,
OLIVIA:	a tart!
OLIVIA:	Her tutu. Gateau –
CHLOE:	chapeau!
OLIVIA:	In the Marzipan Mezzanine,
CHLOE:	her sugar frock cinder block.
OLIVIA:	In animal jelly,
CHLOE:	a crinoline confects ...
OLIVIA:	... such sarcophagus cherries!
CHLOE:	If she crumples ...
OLIVIA:	when she wilts ...
IN UNISON:	*"To the Bin!"*

VI

CHLOE:	Look what I found.
OLIVIA:	
Chloe:	Maybe it's a tiny eye ... ?
OLIVIA:	
OLIVIA:	No. A freshwater pearl.
CHLOE:	Cyclopean.

OLIVIA:	*Fallen.*
CHLOE:	Come undone –
OLIVIA:	from the *ruined* corset ...
	of the Butler's Gap-Toothed Mistress.
CHLOE:	Let's hide it again.
OLIVIA:	Hm. Where?
CHLOE:	Maybe in the Pantry of Rats?
OLIVIA:	No.
CHLOE:	
OLIVIA:	How about under twenty mounds of unspun straw?
CHLOE:	
OLIVIA:	Or under twenty sullen mattresses?
CHLOE:	
OLIVIA:	
CHLOE:	But.
OLIVIA:	What.
CHLOE:	But. What if no one ever finds it?
OLIVIA:	Oh.
OLIVIA:	Well.
CHLOE:	Well.

VII

CHLOE:	The Mother said the Spinster speaks with the dead.
OLIVIA:	Sir Frothwattle said the Spinster has no husband because she talks funny.

That's why she rents Hermione's attic ...

Lady Bailey said the Spinster once had a sister ...

CHLOE: I always wanted a sister!

OLIVIA: ... who pricked herself with a needle.

CHLOE: And then they put her in the dark large box.
OLIVIA: In the dark large box.

VIII

CHLOE'S SONG: My cousin is a tea cozy.
                  I always wanted a sister.

                  She got herself into trouble.
                  "Always catching themselves on fire –

                  those naughty crinolines," said the Father
                  of Chins. "A head on her

                  would be a non sequitur."
                  You cannot see the narrator in the mirror

                  because she is not her.
                  Sometimes I am just a cushion.

IX

OLIVIA:	In the Lady's Chamber.
CHLOE:	Where you look.

OLIVIA:	Everywhere it's just ...
CHLOE:	*Pins.*

And Cushions!

OLIVIA:	*(Sigh) Pins!*
CHLOE:	Yes.

"Cylindrical stalks thick at the lust-
rous head."

CHLOE:	*And Cushions!*
OLIVIA:	Oh, yes.

"Cherubic and enfolding. Enswelled, and sin-
uous bejewelled with cherry or pearl, edgings trimmed
in fine velveteen fourrure."

CHLOE:	Even the smallest eye,
OLIVIA:	weeps silken thread.

X

OLIVIA:	Today is my birthday.
CHLOE:	Today is *my* birthday.

OLIVIA:	*Eleven Squalid Walrus Wishbones!*

CHLOE:	*Eleven Conches' Sonorous Paunches!*
OLIVIA:	*Eleven Pinstriped Paddywhacks!*
CHLOE:	*Eleven Conspicuous Custard Cups!*
OLIVIA:	*Eleven Vexing Vole Vignettes!*

CHLOE:	No – thirteen. Thirteen Vexing Vole Vignettes!
OLIVIA:	Thirteen.
CHLOE:	Eleven plus two – don't forget the Spinster.
OLIVIA:	Okay. But that's only twelve.
CHLOE:	No.

When she works, you can see both of her
in the looking glass.

One, the front. One, the back.

CHLOE:	Well.
	What do you want to do?

OLIVIA:	Well,
	what do you.

CHLOE:	Maybe she'll let us play
	in the Attic.

XI

OLIVIA'S SONG:	The Spinster's reflection handles animal ribs,
	to untangle flax, with cylindrical tines
	for aligning, or blending
	the worsted spectrum. And hackling

boards with blackthorn thorns, both
by wheel and drop spindle. The Devil's

Work. A weight on one end,
and a hook on the other –

the wool is attached
and twisted by hand

to create a single strand. Unlike
wool, silk has neither scales

nor crimp. Then the language of
bobbins, metronomic in her

goes: "Clackety-whir, clackety-whir,"
spouting the nonsense of swans.

XII

CHLOE: The Purple Daughter says the Spinster has magic powers.
OLIVIA: *She can turn one thing into another.*

CHLOE: Just like priests.
OLIVIA: Yes.

CHLOE: Or snipers.
OLIVIA: Oh?

CHLOE: That's why she will live forever.
OLIVIA: Yes.

Well then. What shall we bring her?

CHLOE: *Sapphires!*

            ...

CHLOE: *You hear that?*
OLIVIA: Yes.
CHLOE: It's coming from outside ...

OLIVIA: *The Violet Sellers!*

CHLOE: *Hollering ghastly ...*

OLIVIA: *from their gashly ...*

CHLOE: *Ruby Wagon of Lard.*

XIII

CHLOE: Sometimes they get to wear diamonds.
OLIVIA: Yes.

CHLOE: A diamond is a daughter.
CHLOE: A daughter, hatched,

OLIVIA: from a gilded looking glass.
CHLOE: Yes.

OLIVIA: A looking glass likes to arrange her daughters.

CHLOE: Among Champagne Girls
OLIVIA: who hold their hand-mirrors for them. "Thereby –"

CHLOE:	"taught to love …"
OLIVIA:	"only those who love them back."
OLIVIA:	They are not for us.
CHLOE:	They are not for us.

...

OLIVIA:	The Spinster will lend a gilded thread
CHLOE:	to string us together.
OLIVIA:	Your porcelain hands connect to …
CHLOE:	your prompt bisque shoes.
OLIVIA:	We could borrow her spindle …
CHLOE:	
OLIVIA:	*O Magnificent stilt!*
CHLOE:	I don't know.
	Won't we stumble … ?
OLIVIA:	Oh yes. How we'll tilt.
CHLOE:	
OLIVIA:	But how shall we dress?
CHLOE:	In rhinestones!
OLIVIA:	*Oh yes.*

From the rhinoceros.

OLIVIA:	The one stomping his feet
CHLOE:	in that old wooden crate that keeps falling apart.

CHLOE:	The ones that make you feel.
OLIVIA:	*Something else –*

CHLOE:	Then Awkward and Lumpful, across the whole earth,

together we shall dance
the Rhinoceros Waltz!

OLIVIA:	*as we imagine ...*

CHLOE:	*we must.*

Letter I:
Intermission, the Image
Phenakistoscope Poem

The Phenakistoscope ... Imagine some movement or other, for example a dancer's or a juggler's performance, divided up and decomposed into a certain number of movements ... The twenty little figures, representing the decomposed movement of a single figure, are reflected in a mirror placed in front of you ... Each little figure has availed himself of nineteen others. On the card it spins and its speed makes it invisible; in the mirror, seen through the spinning window, it is motionless, executing on the spot all the movements that are distributed between all twenty figures. *The number of pictures that can thus be created is infinite.*

CHARLES BAUDELAIRE, "The Philosophy of Toys," Trans. Jonathan Mayne (italics added)

...

Each and every one of her,
The same as her, or nearly. "And, so near –"
Each one is a lithograph of her.
Each one is just close enough to hear.
Each one with her paper coat, horsehair.

Twenty of her move in unison.
Nineteen hers, facing her procession.
To almost touch the cloth coat of the one
In front, but then she must move, then her motion
Might enrage or estrange us. Untouched,

The daughters made of paper always follow.
We can't tell which is the original.
So, daughters in the phenakistoscope
Tilt our twenty heads to the left: "Go!"
And when she tilts her head: as if we know

That in her image "Could she know for sure."
She shifts, or shoves – *"Take this,"* as if to share –
To catch and hold her tight, imagine – there!
(Winding string tight 'round her wrist.) Ask her!
"Do you like to be looked at?" at Intermission.

Letter J:
Little Jill Horner and the Sugar Maids

I

Mother'd said it, "Order it,"

whatever we wanted.

Fetched from that place of voices and filled with confections.
In this way, my brother and I call it forth.

II

All the cooks are here in the diner.
They rise up and stare at the family.
White hats hover at the porthole behind where the food is being born.

A *star!* Brother imitates the Butter Boy:
"Hey, careful with that knife you might
suddenly harm the Girl in the Marmalade Jar!"

A spoon cranes its neck beyond its reflection.
At eye level, the belt buckle of the Cardboard Cowboy Man Stand
glints by the till but my brother has to reach up to thumb it.

"But the cream is, the cream is, not performing well!"
says the mother at the eggy tag of the waitress.

Boy Made of Elbows pulls crooked face.
Still, I'll turn any who harm him "into a mule!"
Then fists were his or mine could make me look –
"Resist."

But, well, the mother, "Order,"
said it.

III

Back in their departments the cooks snip portraits
of Sugar Maids from tiny paper packets.
Clip them. Pinned to that greasy wall, slant rows
from which the maids are heard. Are heard

fainter than breath breathing in a room, murmuring.
Sound white voices from their rows.
In the diner, the confections are squirming.
Now all the cooks have gone.

IV

The Sugar Maids summon forth the cakes:

beneath the glass bubble their own breath sips
their pastel gloss, nips it – and presses back
against a kind in glass under the meniscus of a township.

Now watch. Forehead at the cold dome,
iced surface dips, slip down pink sides, to drip.
A better girl would well not wanted, well.
None notice that the pies are swelling.

Letter K:
Knowing

Key:

"I must forget the dormitory of wood."

Knob:

"The blindfold never complains."

Kite:

"Lifting my elbows with the breath of dogs
and trailing rubies. Lie still! Lie still."

Knee socks:

"We are capable."

Letter L:
Line Dance

An Inkstress just like Auntie Iambe limps across Main Street.

She interrupts the traffic with the shuffle of estranged feet.

The trucks honk and the wheels screech as they stop and wait, "We'll see ..."

If she'll pause in the middle, or will head "Off!" to the sea.

Her left step clops in a dead stop. From which the right one swings –

And pulls the left one "forwards ..." our invisible lace strings.

Letter M:
Meaning, a Triptych of Translations

Before we were narrative, we were boots and vertigo.
ROBERT MAJZELS

If I am no longer capable of translating or metaphorizing, I become silent and I die.
JULIA KRISTEVA, *Black Sun: Depression and Melancholia*

...

I. Dew-Daughter

He caught water in a net of air. At leaf hinge, it gathers there. And rounding
within its walls a sister with translucent skin whom he has never met before.
A room that is also his eye. The water chamber swells: to this exact moment
in which it is a perfect globe is also the moment of its falling a line cuts this
streak in air. Tiny river, as it translates: *tear.*

II. The Girl Who Was a Drawing (Or, Ekphrastic Poem on the Letter L)

Lustrous buckled little shoes, ashen-spleened.
"Step. Step. Step."

Tiny freckle on a freckle,
she is a liquid drop of ink. Beside herself,

she makes a line, "I am my own
sisters." Rattle, rattle

go the dollhouse walls. The little line
goes on and on. And as she goes,

she is more line,
more her. The ungloved hand directs her,

a crayon or a quill, drawing.
Voices in air she swallows, faking.

She is a Chorus on a Marching-Road,
a Phone line, or that

Exactly Architect who was
supposed to be, to build "Something."

Her forehead, blue-black
like the surface of sleep water, arrives

at the Mean Wall that is as long as
she is tall. The Wall

has windows or teeth or mirrors.
Perpendicular, her elbow meets it at its heel

and latches. "Perhaps we are a Letter L."
"Beloved."

III. Confectionery

Monday, I am a bead of blackest icing scowl. Tuesday, a drop and a drop;
two pearls birthed from a dark-lipped oyster, or chickens nestling cherubic
and puddling. Wednesday, I was three rotundas of sugar, a crusting crinoline
hem, this trio of velvet ravens. Thursday, they will call me a row. "A row!"
Friday, I am called by loudspeaker to assemble in a police lineup, a pageant –
such unusual salesgirls at twilight.

Letter N:
The Cameo Essay – Towards a Poetics of Nonsense
An Ekphrasis

Cameo, A Woman's Head. Onyx or Obsidian on Gold, Bohemia, 1930s.
Black Swan Antiques, Whyte Ave., Edmonton, 1991–2023

…

Unlike the nineteenth-century nonsense poets, the dadaists and surrealists were willing to invert the rules of poetic form....
    ... Nonsense as a critical activity is and is about change; is an aspect of and is about the ongoing nature of the social process.
    SUSAN STEWART, *Nonsense: Aspects of Intertextuality in Folklore and Literature*

You could say that form is learning.
    LISA ROBERTSON, "On Form"

…

The woman's miniature head is speaking.

From that obsidian tablet, "From
Bavaria," which rests in the palm crook
as a book would.

Her head is speaking in your palm
from its lustrous black placard of unrest, lit
and bordered in a delicate casket of real gold.
Overheard, stored in the tiny cameo
you hold, and fashioned in the style of those
once commissioned by the wealthy
or the grieving.
The realistic impression
of her presence is a carved relief

formed of pallid bone, then set onto a darker background
of contrasting colour. Sunken
it holds ink. Its active recess
postpones its visibility
in order to render her
seen, or her divisibility imposes this. *"I don't know what you mean*

By your way,"
the Red Queen said,
before ordering the beheading
of that well-intending girl
(the one who knew that if she got
the rhyme wrong she would not be,
or could be instead some other girl
named "Mabel"). How she struggled.
What to do when her ankles
and elbows monstrous wouldn't fit the room
(if witnessed this would mean
an embarrassment). And it seemed
that everybody's words
had the power to hurt her. Uniformly. Her ankle-strap
shoes sodden with salt water,
she took Things seriously,
consulted talking Tiger Lily and Rose,
and damaged men, and that Caterpillar
who demanded: "Who are *you*?" –
and she even questioned language itself
regarding these and other
matters, such as how one thing
becomes another, not to mention
her conversations with her feline familiar.
(Often left with no choice
but to address only aspects
of his head, and how he comprehended
the social mechanics

of hiding the body – {"*I mean –*
I beg your pardon ..." she said and said.}
to be perceived,
if not accurately, then at least
unobtrusively.)
And she could only silence the Red Queen, if briefly, by uttering, *"Nonsense!"*

In a voice most persnickety,
the Red Queen (whose tarts
had recently been carried off), had insisted,
"all the ways about here belong to *me* ..."
and scholars also bicker as to whether
Henry VIII was the very first to say it.
Said it twice, and artfully, "Off with it,"
for two of his six wives,
while the original beheaded queen
is believed to have been Mary
of Scots. Her murder, authorized
by her cousin Elizabeth, for having had such dark thoughts

Of assassination,
such as that of Marie
Antoinette, whose extermination, by her own
people, also by decapitation,
was predicated and based
upon the desecration of her
reputation. Though she never did
utter what they said she said
about "... Cake!" nevertheless,
all the women were forever imitating
her illicit fashions. A patron
of the arts, Marie had adopted
the orphan of a chambermaid, and imported
poor children with whom her own children
could play, so that they would

not lack in humility (and her last words
were purported to be an apology
to her Executioner, Sanson, mortified
for having accidentally stepped on his foot
"Monsieur, I didn't mean
it"). Still, the main reason for the fervour
of their ill favour was apparently curated
by her predilection for dressing
like a kept woman. "A slut," requires re-
form, since a mistress kept might take
some pleasure. As opposed to regal
piousness. Lascivious. So they insisted,
and paraded the head, severed, devilish,
of her dear friend the Princesse
de Lamballe outside of Marie's cell
where she knelt in hay.
While they cut her hair she prayed in a white petticoat.

Once Marie was beheaded, the gravediggers
took a lunch break,
which allowed a young sculptor,
Marie Grosholtz, who later became
Madame Tussaud, the opportunity
to take a wax imprint of Marie's face
for a death mask.
When later exhumed, Marie's body
had mostly deteriorated,
except for her two somewhat beloved garters, which remained in perfect condition,

Whereas, Medusa loved *absolutely.*

Remember, Medusa was not
always a monster. Somehow,
the only mortal
among three sisters, the only

chaste one, a devoted priestess
of the goddess Athena, at that.
And once "beautiful."

Intending to annoy
his competitor, with whom he battled
to become Athens's patron,
as a military tactic (though perhaps
also an amusement,
since he was among innumerable gods
whose formative erotic conquests
fetishized overpowerment – itself
a form of the sacredness
of violence such that even gods
delighted in it)
Poseidon raped Medusa in the centre
of Athena's temple.
Discovering this,
Athena, who loved to play
with infinity, transformed Medusa
into a monument of inexorable
solitude,

Banished, her hair made
of live snakes and her skin that
restless greenish hue, now marked by Athena's questionably
attributed punishment, and deformed. Medusa's
gaze – for which she is known best,
and considered reprehensible on its behalf –
would turn male onlookers
into stone (unless, of course
she was meant merely as metaphor –
for the repugnant audacity
of that woman whose look can undo
when it says – "I do not
desire you") except for Perseus

the hero who crept upon her
while she slept. And slayed her.
He relieved her hissing mind
of subjectivity,

Or, absolving her head of its unendurable
body,
Perseus then paraded her,
severed, and wielded
inimitably at all enemies,
as if to say, "Fuckers, get a load
of this!" (before surrendering it
in deference to Athena
to be placed, in relief, and forever,
upon and as her shield). And turned Medusa into a weapon,

Or into art.

Gods understand the power of beauty.
Real, magnificent, indomitable.
Desire, sublime and resented it.
On certain days was she thankful
for it.

It was not quite
as different as she thought. *"To become monstrous –"*

Ambiguous, and in excess,
was familiar. How odd.

Prior, when she had been
so exceedingly magnificent she could feel
them ill at ease on its behalf – their discomfort, which, all decided,
she was the cause of it – and now coupled with
their desire to own her; now
Their fear is eerily similar –

palpable. This version
of the compulsion
to own her, transformed,
nonsensical, into the compulsion
to destroy her. Contrary, to gossip, she never had a tail
though she understood the paradox
of the need to be seen,
and its danger
asked a series of common
questions: to ever trust a man again,
and if ever, which;
but for her
the stakes got higher – could she ever trust
a god? –

Or a woman.
Some days in here so quiet, peaceful without others are so much more dangerous

("I need someone to talk to")

that did she sometimes choose
that hollow grotto its depression hidden within the bedrock lesser anguish
and retreat
within it.

So few visitors though she always tossed the incriminating takeaway boxes
and clinking rubbish when someone turned up.

"Don't look at me –"

Historians sometimes forget
to remember.
Medusa was never
a man-hater, and if a metaphor
were to follow her, further, and then further still,

Into that solitary cavern where she sits and sits "trying not to (be seen
to) need anyone" – *then,*

perhaps not to stone, but into sculpture, was how she turned him. A way
"To keep you, my beloved, is to turn you into art." Where, "There, maybe a man
can hurt me less."
("Any man
can be made

to fit
the shape of it.") Though not nearly

As intimate,
the listening other she imagines in her chamber. And would write to.
Though Medusa knew,

The other woman in the cave   is, and
"Is neither me nor you"

when she turned to her apostrophe and said: "*See –*
I too can make a god."

Letter O:
Onwards
To and From, a Dialogue

To:

"Sparrow and flight inseparable until."

From:

"The silo's shadow gapes back – becoming is the tall
and talling giant of my childhood this feeling is bigger I could show you."

Letter P:
Polly Pollen

The nineteenth century saw the creation of a tradition that saw childhood ...
JUDITH ROWBOTHAM, *Good Girls Make Good Wives: Guidance for Girls in Victorian Fiction*

"Oh dear, what nonsense I'm talking!"
      Just at this moment her head struck against the roof of the hall.
LEWIS CARROLL, *Alice's Adventures in Wonderland*

...

"Quick! Tie Her up –"
said the Custard Cup,

"With Him-Ribbon."
"Or, hold Her

down by Her-hair,"
chortled the Important Porter. Fundamentally, as-

king in a voice most queenly:
"Where goes that Polly,

with her hundred hats!"
chimed, conspicuous, the Catalytic Cat.

"Now, bind Her tight. That She won't stir –"
"But, Sire, still She stares and stares."

Letter Q:
"One Final Touch-Up Before the Coronation ..."
Queen Bee Poem

I. "Once Upon a Time, There Was a Beautiful Queen"

What noise does a Queen make?
Daughters.

At what moment did you become Queen?
Birth is not a choice. I cannot say I liked it.

When does the Queen's reign begin?
In murder. ("Just like Cleopatra," I killed my sister.)

Tell us about sisters.
I'd be lying if I said she came at me first.

And, began?
Then I awoke in the Tenement of Astonishment.

II. *Work Song: Punk Rock Chorus Line*

"Wax Work, Nuns' Work for Young Gentlewomen"

Daughter, the Swaddler; Daughter, the Coddler.
One, Sister of Tantrums; One, Her Royal Taster.
One Sister, Her Apron; One is Her High Diaper.
To predigest breakfasts for Her Blessèd Highness.

Maid, Her Materials; Maid of the Chamber pot,
To scoop and to shuttle Her Faeces Imperial.
Come, Nursemaids with baskets behind our keen knees.
Our Chorus: *Our Queen is the Best Queen!*

Applause, as She dances in the Ballroom
to signal it's time for the Daughters to groom
and preen her. Dressed in our knee socks of fur.
In jellies sopped with our teeth, we wash Her.

Soon Lady of Fans shall cool the Great Room.
Sister Builders build hexagonal tombs
which double as Nursery, Larder or Pantry,
Wax Factory, Rooming House and Dormitory.
Beauticians-in-Waiting starve Her for mating.
One, Mistress of Blisters, wipes down glossy Babies.
Our crammed tenement doubles as Latrine,
and Frat House agleam, then Sorority Row;
and her Coffin of Sugar. *Our Queen, the Best Queen!*
When She grows old, another will grow.

She would have us remain children forever.
When Workers grow up, we will be Workers.
No strangers can get past the Butler of Pins!
We learn in our sleep. We may even dream.
Our Queen is the Best Queen:

When She dreams of a mind, she dreams us.
Now, see that, without much daughterly fuss,
Her Attendants crowd Her: Her Royal Assassins.

One of us Sisters is Her Executioner.
Soon we will shout *Now it's time* for the Builders
to convert her Boudoir to Mortuary Chamber.

And finally, summon the Highest Priestess!
Undertaker Sister, she'll sweep and she'll sweep
Her Royal Corpse – *Out! Out!* – with the mess
because *Our Queen is the Best Queen.*
When she got too old, we made a new one.
She will be the Best Queen. At last –
none foreign shall get past!

III. The Sex Lives of Queens

A Virgin Queen sleeps in the room with her mother.
Since infancy,

never unaccompanied, nor without a governess
"Always hovering," government in a dress,

well groomed. Queen Victoria, too, craved
privacy, "An hour alone" was her request, at the moment

of her coronation. Akin to Catherine de' Medici,
she, whose contractual nuptials

were scrutinized, bedside, by the King
on the night of her wedding to his son. "A matter of state,"

our nakedness, though they would have preferred
that I possess beauty – (as Cleopatra's

good looks are said to have been a lie,
her chief asset, in fact, was her intellect. She'd speak

of astronomy, while refusing to release
the sac of your earlobe from her teeth) – rather than

appetite. In contrast to Catherine the Great,
vilified for yielding the moat of pearl

to multiple lovers as did kings, I pay
little mind as to who is which of my sons' fathers.

I flounce in blouses of air,
fuck many mothers' sons on high – and only then,

that once or twice,
darling daughters, do I ever leave your side.

IV. The Personal Effects of the Queen

After the death of the King,
eight fashion dolls dressed in elaborate mourning garb
were discovered among the belongings of Catherine de' Medici.

On Mother's nightstand,
no glass slipper. But a single memento, the tombstone
of Father, his detached phallus gilded in amber dust

(Perhaps this is why they fear us).

And a looking glass that captures
the eyes of her detractors.

V. Conditions for Impeachment of the Monarch

i	If her Beauty, no longer Inspires.
ii	If she is Barren, Barren, Barren.
iii	If the Sons she spawns are deemed Lazy, Dim-Witted, Lustless or Stinky.
iv	If she refuses to silence in Her dank Queen Cell,
v	Murder may be deemed Most Economical.

VI. Interview with the Daughters: *Chorus*

Who is responsible for the suffering of your Mother?
Some say Nature, others call it the Higher Power.

If you had Three Wishes?
Can you help me make my Mother live forever –

(*Or at least until I can save her*).

VII. Mausoleum Lullaby: In Memoriam for My Death
for my Daughter, the Undertaker Bee

In the Powder Room of the Violet, bleeding

Its moat of sugar-water

Bring me Mad Marmalades.

Nostalgist of the Rooming House, I don't have as much time left

As I would like. My coterie, I covet. I confect,   "Further,"

Further, my Fatherless –

Daughters. When the man in white smiles bare-handed, only a mother

Can die.   A Queen is a longer dreaming. Reverie of scarves

Tied to a garter belt tied to a noose   Extinguished. The hands of a mob girlishly

Kept me warm in winter. Soon, only outliers will still reek of me.

                Men of Science say a Queen has no place

(When I was beautiful you acted kindly to me. I can remember every face

Of those who harmed, indispensable   I, once.

Errant tableaux.   Chandelier, when Chambermaids were my hands

Light Collectors

You cannot even tell where the light comes from)

                For interiority.   *Come home.*

Letter R:
Requiem for Our Hunting Fathers

Foreheads of men have bled where no wounds were.
> WILFRED OWEN, "Strange Meeting"

Violence of rhyme because it is violence that makes rhyme.
> HENRI MESCHONNIC, "Rhyme and Life," Trans. Gabriella Bedetti

...

At the Arm Farm
The Farmers farmed Arms
Harvesting a Far Arm Army.

Arm Farmers do their best
To knit Vests for Guests' chests:
"My Best Guest," he firmly addressed

"While our vast Arms, invested
Can't dress you, Armless –
Nevertheless, this Vest is for you."

Letter S:
The Story of the Striped Cravat and the Striped Uniform
An Ekphrasis

Thus Spake the Stripes ...

Pallor:

"In single file. Why I have to have to speak
first. My echo, my echo. I forgot, no, failed, to memorize his face.
Now, keep marching!"

Sable:

"The ancestors moan from the chesterfield upholstered
with a swath of women's silvering hairs. My pallid shadow
remembers forwards, and unstable. In the pantry beside the
room of such similar proportions within the poorly lit mansion."

Letter T:
PART ONE – "(Never) The Time for Beauty"

Les Demimondaines, Poem III

Then, Years of Darkness. Thin-ankled, the days dimmed, wincing, and rationed remembered light. Shadows latched, and fastening to all objects once bright, curdle. Cupcake-Shadow, Tailpipe-Shadow, Shadow-Shadow. Nights howled from the Bankrupt trough of your bald neighbour's hat. Everyone was saving everything for The Effort.

Mornings, we line up in the factory. In numbered rows shift rickety chairs, on the hour on the hour, and hoard scraggly mutt sunbeams. Grumble Man in the Checkered Vest stands on an overturned milk crate, bellows into the loudspeaker patched with tape: *Never the Time For ...* Now we fashion only *un*decorated porcelain. For the Effort. Hunch-shouldered. Each day: The New Forbidden Words. After she went away.

At first, we looked for her everywhere. I was not old before. Plaid Petra uncrosses her legs as a fuchsia underskirt hem flickers at her ankles. *Never the Time For ... !* On Wednesday, I watched him fuss with his pant leg, almost caught his eye. Did I? And was seen or remembered remembering being seen my face burns. *Never the Time For ...* Yesterday, when the featherless magpie took off aslant, teetering on one foot: the exact angle of her cheekbone. We no longer say the Word.

Terror Number Two: fear that shiveringly becomes giddiness bewilders when we steal teacups and saucers from the factory vault. Copped and coveted, we stash stolen housewares under threadbare cardigans. We walk slowly and talk mostly nonsense. Who called me stupid, stupid girl. Above all, remain calm. We remain calm.

Nightly, Dolly's mother and sisters crouch in candlelight painting Dolly on scoffed china. With pilfered pigments and stink paraffin, I among them. Says the Sister of the Gap Tooth: *I paint her green-yellow scarf, a flapping, flag-like, that surrounds and exceeds her.* Says the Sister of the Club Foot: *To dot and flit,*

lines, and her infinite golden crinoline akin to scales. Sister the Widower lets one tulip droop but holds the other two upright with her brush tip never (*Never!*) looks away until they are dry. Tomboy Sister dyed her hair black in the abandoned gas station restroom, traded kisses with the bearded trench coat for a ticket to Away but came Right Back.
Sister Tomboy only paints the eyes.

For the Effort.

We began to fall in love with her variations. Over and over is that is remember. When Sister the Widower sneezed, the accident the splash made *What a pretty globe, her scarf bubbling, erupts: a frog's eye!* When Mother set out to outline Dolly's hat and was crying so she could barely see. So her line slipped, exceeded and exceeds her. Then Dolly's sudden chapeau becomes also a foghorn so that she can find us.

Punk rock philosophers *What is a daughter!* smoke pirated cigarettes on the fire escape. In the Alley of Childhood, whispers: *Dolly in Drag! Dolly the Dunce-Cap! Delirious, Dreamingly, Demon-Daughter!* We debate, does the wound reside in shadow or in remembered light itself smoke rings come untied, no matter, into nothing, nest, or into Shadow-Shadow whispering, *Dolly Varden, Dolly Varden.*

Name me the one who dares tax the trout – obedient, dowdy-grey where visible, his private underside roils with iridescent pinkness! Or, who dares incarcerate the crankle-clawed crab on the sea floor. Witnessed by few or none, and buried in sand with only her eyes exposed. Her back, a vision of grandeur, gasps, her carapace reddens in sad fantastic patches. For when it is time.
On her back she carries the sea anemone.

I should not have told her my hands were burning because then she gave me her gloves.

Letter T:
PART TWO – Trading Beauty Secrets with the Dead: The Dolly Varden Essay

Les Demimondaines, Poem IV

Dolls should be seen. They should be gathered. They should be.
With all my heart.

> GERTRUDE STEIN, *How to Write*

PART ONE: DOLLS ARE NOT FOR CHILDREN

I

"But they are not for children," insisted artist Lotte Pritzel. When she found herself. Time and time again, moved. To create her.

Strange Dolls made of wax.

II

After viewing the exhibition of wax Dolls created by Lotte Pritzel in Munich, 1913, poet Rainer Maria Rilke was moved. To define their *unnatural* natures.

III

Lotte, whose husband prescribed opium for her artistic "distress" doted night after night in her studio. The minutiae of their tiny faces. Her "Puppen für die Vitrine" or "Wax Dolls for the Showcase." Morphine. Her stolid gaze, composed. Then she adorned their alarmingly or parodically overthin bodies ornately. Dr. Gerhard Pagel once commented on their "deranged child-like expressions," however,

Lotte would only ever explain them as *"creatures of herself."*

IV

Lotte travelled in fashionable circles, the Munich Bohème, then off to Berlin. Yet, wherever she went, Lotte refused to fashion her creatures of herself for fame or fortune although they went for high prices. As for any explanation of their natures, she had neither use nor intention.

V

In his *Duino Elegies*, Rainer Maria Rilke imagined children as
the "toy" that "a grief" once received, when grief "was still
quite small," and "during one of its long convalescences."

To presumably revisit us, *grief,* throughout our lifetimes.

VI

Rilke was unsettled by Lotte's avant-garde "Artist Dolls."
Captivated, he wrote at length about this encounter.

Either because they were oddly fashioned from the ethereal
substance of wax – homely and unhomely, they appeared to
glow – or because they were intended for an audience of adults,
he believed that "the precondition of their origin would be that

the world of childhood is past."

He thought Lotte's dolls had "finally outgrown the understanding,
the involvement, the joy and sorrow of the child."

And so, they provoked him, enormously.

VII

Each Doll costumed in frothing resplendence. Handmade
one at a time, as if her body parted from within her attire,
privately withdrawing or retreating into luminous thinness.
Her "peculiar" skin, at once opaque and translucent, as if infinite.

Near intimate, ineluctably alien; if beauty, then.

VIII

Lotte's Dolls. How alarmingly "independent, grown up."

Creatures of herself, so "prematurely old."

And Rilke, distressed by their "indifferent permanence."

IX

The Wax Dolls of Lotte Pritzel were born. In an era in which
women and girls. *Were becoming.* Both market and workforce.
The shift from mannequins to live models in the fashion industry
went on to inspire fashion photography and the representation
of living female celebrities in the form of dolls.

X

Their faces do seem luminescent, beguile. Mostly female, adult,
at once ageless, they erupt from their souls in gaunt profiles
whose lines extend outwards into the theatricality, the grand
swooping gestures of their vestments of brocade, of cambric,
of velvet.

Lotte was also a Costume and Set Designer, inspired by the grace
of the – often undernourished – female dancers of the time. She built
sets and costumes into which the Dolls might fit, constructed
costumes and sets that might house the Dolls. Sometimes stringed,
Lotte's Dolls, in turn, went on to inspire movements and costumeries
of living female dancers. If beauty, then.

XI

Lotte began by designing Dolls with movable limbs. As her Doll-making practice evolved, she began to make the Dolls static.

Then, she placed them behind glass cloches and cases, and would direct the staging of photographs taken of them.

XII

This distance between viewer and Doll created by the glass, and the distance emphasized by the photographs were, as Sara Ayres observes, all part of the artwork and reminiscent of Victorian taxidermy practices.

A review of Lotte's exhibition from 1920 likens her Dolls to "peculiar insects, fixed and pinned in their display cases." The act of exhibition on exhibit, our looking.

Viewers described the Dolls as "androgynous." Some described them as erotic, while others deemed their natures to be "sterile" and "sexless."

Viewers purported that they all looked "related," although interestingly, they belonged to different "races." They seemed to exist amongst themselves harmoniously, "without hierarchy."

Walter Benjamin commented upon them. Upon meeting her Dolls, some were reminded of how Benjamin had borrowed from the lives of certain women who walked among the glass arcades to create his metaphor of the Prostitute, which, abstracted from the walking women, posited that "love for the Prostitute is the apotheosis of empathy with the commodity."

Exuding a certain "self-sufficiency," Lotte and her Dolls,
resisting interpretation.

XIII

The Wax Dolls of Lotte compelled Rilke to return to his memory
of having once lavished affections on toys as a child, so much so that
his toys seemed to become *involved* in the human world.

Within a condition of intimacy, his interiority had been safe with her;
penetrated, witnessed, unendangered.

He recalled that moment when his childhood doll would insist
upon her alterity, retract:

then forever retain her separateness.

That epiphanic instant between doll and child in which,
independent from his mind, she no longer *belonged*

to his longing.

XIV

The Doll who became uninvolved with "the joy and sorrow
of Rilke's childhood. Perhaps, rather than outgrowing
his toys, she outgrew him.

Rilke claimed that this universal experience of children – forced to
return to our loneliness on behalf of our dolls' intractable
indifference towards us –

could cause our very first awareness, or in fact be the genesis, of
"the heart pause *which could spell death* ..."

XV

He went on to explain that when, later in life, we remember how
she abandoned us into the solitude of subjectivity,

some of us then translate this traumatic revelation as:

"The suspicion that one cannot be loved."

XVI

The "horrible, dense forgetfulness" of the doll of childhood
emerges *at exactly the same time*

as the child's discovery of his (*sic*) actual "hatred" for her,

Which "*must always have been an unconscious part of our
connection*" with her,

thought Rilke.

XVII

In 1924, the Surrealist photographer Hans Bellmer received
a box full of his childhood toys from his mother when his father,
with whom he had always had conflict, fell ill. Broken dolls and
sugar pigeons. Full of grief, he travelled to Paris.

During this time, he visited an exhibition of Lotte Pritzel's Wax
Dolls. Provoked by her work, he began to work with increased
emphasis on representations of representations of dolls,
in his own art. Apparently, Lotte advised him generously.

Hans constructed deconstructed assemblages of doll-based female
figures from found materials such as broom handles, nuts and bolts.

One doll had a space in her stomach in which an entire panorama could be inserted.

XVIII

Together with his wife, Margarete, Hans Bellmer invented his unnamed "Artificial Girl."

He too took photographs of her. Then he hand-painted them.

XIX

Dolls or doll-like, "They were created for the higher purpose," said Hans, of expressing a critique "of the idealized, fascist German body."

Their doll-based bodies, disarticulated, detached. All their gazes averted, or, simply, eyeless.

His fragmented doll bodies were represented as if this fragmentary detachment was part of their nature. Their marked bodies. His conflation of worship and derision.

Some posit that his collection *Die Puppe* may express, in part, his critique of the System of the Father. Therein, daughters eyeless and abstracted; the Daughter a metaphor within a wider battle.

Noting that Hans's female figures were created to be incapable of looking or loving back, Surrealist poet Paul Éluard was moved to write prose poems to them:

"It's a girl – where are her eyes? –
It's a girl, it is my desire."

XX

Hans deployed female dolls as what he termed his "poetic stimulator" –
vehicle or machine, through which to generate self-reflection. Moved
by Hans's dolls, fellow Surrealist artists Man Ray and Salvador Dalí
went on to create their own artworks housed by the bodies of young,
erotically charged female dolls. The invention of our incompleteness,
her body as our narrator. Ventriloquy.

Lotte's Wax Dolls for the Showcase, "letting themselves
be dreamed ..." dreamed Rilke.

XXI

Doll and child: newly strangers, bound by death.

Doll of Mortality. Doll of Self-Love. Doll of Sublimity, she. Responsible.
For our expulsion.

And so, "We took our bearings from the doll,"
Rilke proposed.

PART TWO: "WE TOOK OUR BEARINGS FROM THE DOLL"

I make them do exactly what I want,
I sit them down in knitted frocks like dolls

who beg me to forgive them – and I do!
I finally forgive them! Only joking.

    SELIMA HILL, "The Dolls"

I

Defined as miniature representations of the human form, dolls
have continuously puzzled archaeologists regarding their natures.

Toy historian Lois Kuznets reminds us that in the effort to determine
the purpose of certain miniaturized human figures excavated from
ancient ruins, time and time again archaeologists could only base their
hypotheses – *But what is her nature?* – on the location in which the
dolls were found.

Since dolls maintain their silence, it is often otherwise impossible to
determine whether these small humanoid sculptures were created for
the purpose of children's play, or for their very first purpose recorded
in human history:

that of worship.

II

The "Louvre Doll" – a term of endearment for the world-famous
Ancient Binding Doll or Bewitchment Figurine housed in the Louvre
Museum Collection – tells many stories in her silence.

Time and time again, removed from the showcase to be housed
in storage, she is believed to have originated in the Antinooupolis
region of Middle Egypt in the third to fourth century. Made of terra-
cotta, she is nine centimetres tall, four centimetres wide. She was
discovered in a clay vase containing herself and a lead tablet upon
which an incantation consisting of twenty-eight lines was inscribed
by an expert hand.

Her body has been pierced through by thirteen long bronze needles.

Beginning with her face: two through each eye, one through her mouth.

Then her body: one for each hand, two for the bottoms of her feet,
one through her brain, one through each ear, one through the middle
of her chest between her breasts and two through her sexual organs.
She kneels, leaning back slightly. Her hands and feet forever bound.

Undressed, once she belonged, most likely, to the household shrine at the
altar from which the gods were addressed within the heart of the home.
She herself was also a shrine.

III

Had archaeologists not also discovered the inscribed tablet along with
her, the tablet which bears the poetic incantation establishing the purpose
of her creation (which in itself seems to have doubled as punishment), the
Louvre Doll would have been indistinguishable from any other Bewitch-
ment Figurine impaled with long needles, a practice through which one
commonly addressed the gods. And with such *reverent* hatred:

To, please, destroy my enemy.

IV

Translated, the magical instructions on the tablet are *a love spell.*

V

Sarapammon, the son of Aréa loved Ptolémaïs. Ptolémaïs, daughter
of Aïas and Origène. Sarapammon would have hired, or been owed
a favour from a religious practitioner or magician who conducted
the spell. The spell is an appeal to the god of deceased Antinoos
who would have assisted in sending a message to chthonic gods
Pluton, Coré-Perséphone-Ereschigal, Adonis, Hermès-Thoth and
Anoubis, and to the spirits of children who died prematurely.

In order to wake Antinoos, and to evoke the affections of his beloved
earthly Ptolémaïs, to pronounce this in the name of the supreme god
Adonis. Sarapammon is Ptolémaïs's attendant; she is the attendant to
the gods. What he longed for.

VI

Sarapammon prayed that his beloved Ptolémaïs be taken, led,
be brought to him, forever loving and submissive unto only himself.
And in this,

that she be bound by death.

VII

The spell begins by invoking the names of the deities, including
Hermès and Perséphone who guard admissions to Hades. The
spell contains this plea:

*That Ptolémaïs not be allowed to eat, nor drink, nor love, nor leave,
nor find rest long from me, Sarapammon.* The plea involves the earth
opening, demons trembling, rivers and rocks coming apart. *If the gods
do this for me, they shall be freed from any encumbrance.*

Beloved Ptolémaïs will be dragged by her hair, by her entrails, until
she does not leave me. That I possess her for my entire life, beloved
and desired by only her.

That she will belong to me.

VIII

You will offer only me, tell me, me only, the thoughts of your mind.

IX

Beautiful Ptolémaïs.

X

And Sarapammon who desired only to touch her across that distance,
if beauty.

Ptolémaïs, pierced with thirteen bronze needles. Ptolémaïs now world-
famous, known as the Louvre Doll since it now owns her.

Bound by death, thirteen bronze needles having become part of her
beauty marked by his desire upon her.

XI

Once she too was spotlit in her showcase, the wax doll in the British
Victoria and Albert Museum, now housed somewhere quietly out of
the way. Born in 1869, she is dressed in the Dolly Varden style,
named after the famous minor character from Charles Dickens's
novel *Barnaby Rudge* (1841).

Like the coquette from the little-read historical novel with whom she shares her name, the waxen Dolly Varden doll is remembered mainly for her lavish costumery. Meticulously dressed, Dolly Varden the literary character, daughter of the locksmith.

She too would sit and sit.

XII

Here she is: garbed in a "dark printed cotton dress over quilted petticoat of maroon silk; white hat with maroon ribbons, dressed by Powell family" to whom she first belonged, and who made the donation of her. If her quiet is resplendent.

Her owner, Letitia Clark (1741–1801), married a London merchant and had a habit of dressing dolls in contemporary fashions, often adorning them in handmade clothing identical to her own. Between a species of play and worship, her female descendants carried on this tradition of dressing her dolls, and their dolls' dolls, until 1912. Letitia's descendants loved adorning her doll-descendants with accessories connected to contemporary pastimes, such as croquet mallets. One was dressed, as did many women of her time, in full mourning garb for Queen Victoria.

XIII

In his famous essay "The Philosophy of Toys" ("Morale du Joujou," 1853) poet and enfant terrible Charles Baudelaire claimed that

"the toy is the child's earliest initiation into art, or rather it is
the first concrete example of art;

and when maturity intervenes, the most rarefied example will not satisfy his mind with the same enthusiasm, nor the same fervent conviction."

In the same essay, he affectionately conjures what he presumed to be the widespread compulsion of children:

the image of children who rattle and shake their toys in the quest to find their souls. Then, for these children who find no evidence of sentience in their impenetrable playthings, nor the capacity for thought or empathy:

"This is the beginning of melancholy and gloom."

XIV

Letitia's waxen Dolly Varden doll, frequently removed from view, confined to sit in storage quarters in order. To make room for more fresh, recent, more fashionable exhibits.

XV

Baudelaire celebrated children's play with toys, especially when liberated from rule-bound play. When young girls play with dolls, he presumed, such play is of a lesser nature, since girls' play with dolls must surely consist of the mere imitation of scripts for pre-scribed adult female behaviour.

He would never take a wife, he swore, who had ever "played"
in such a way.

XVI

As a child, Baudelaire and his mother had been invited to visit the
manor of a wealthy woman. As it happened, she reserved a room –
its sole purpose to house the most unimaginably magnificent
toys for occasions such as this – when she was visited by children
who would grow up to be good boys.

She beckoned him to select *any one he desired.*

For the rest of his life, Baudelaire recalled her with reverence.
Madame Panckoucke,
his "toy fairy."

At the same time, he recalled his mother with disdain,

scandalized, for having instructed him to exchange the toy
he wanted to love – more magnificent than he could have imagined –
for an imaginable one, less costly, less ostentatious, explicably
less beautiful.

XVII

Baudelaire claimed to be eternally puzzled by children who seem
compelled to destroy their toys.

What "mysterious motive" to direct their "passion against these
tiny objects which imitate humanity."

XVIII

Within innumerable human cultures, the tradition of doll-making
and the tradition of passing dolls down from mother to daughter
are conjoined practices, ubiquitous.

Until the last century and a half, dolls were mainly handmade
with local and natural materials. The mass production and export
of dolls is a more recent phenomenon, first popularized by empires
such as Germany and France in what is known as "the golden age of
doll-making," circa 1850 to 1915. This practice spread also to England
and the US.

The manufacture of innumerable self-resembling dolls also flourished
in Japan, and in China where the creation of porcelain originated.
Some propose that knowledge of porcelain-making was brought
over to Europe by the Venetian explorer Marco Polo. Beatrice Alexander
was the first woman to mass-produce dolls in North America.

"Madame Alexander" introduced the Fashion Doll in the US.
Fashion Dolls were first used by European royalty as a way to
ensure that royals remained in the know regarding what belonged
and did not belong in contemporary fashion. As a strategy towards
ensuring their own belonging.

XIX

The pagan or pre-Christian practice of "idolatry," the worship of
a deity through worship of images and objects, *idols*, predates
Christian and Judaic uses of the term: the worship of a false god,
the worship of an object instead of God.

Etymologically, the term was transformed from a description of
worship to a derisive term, which established that prayer itself,
to non-Christian gods, was criminal, scandalous.

XX

The famous Doll Maker Madame Alexander introduced the precursor
or ancestress of Barbie (who was created by a mother for her daughter),
the Fashion Doll, to American markets. Madame was also the first North
American to introduce plastics into their production in the 1960s.
She began with their faces.

XXI

Growing up in New York's Lower East Side, Beatrice lived above
her stepfather's Doll Hospital. Her Jewish father may have been
killed by a Russian pogrom. Her Jewish stepfather had, prior, been
employed as a toy merchant with a pushcart.

Her stepfather spent much of his time repairing the china dolls
owned by wealthy collectors and their children. Delicate as they
were, they were endlessly subjected to damage.

XXII

She began with their faces: their plastic faces now glowed, whitish
or pinkish pearl, near-translucent, and could now withstand –

"I am sorry to break ..." –

a bashing by children.

XXIII

Madame Alexander only started to make dolls during World War I
as a desperate attempt to save her family from financial ruin.

The first doll she made, then reproduced and sold, innumerably, was a beautiful Red Cross Nurse.

Widely considered angelic, if not holy, and dating back to the Middle Ages when nursing was done mostly by nuns, the Healer of the Red Cross. Everyone could always call her "Sister."

PART THREE: A WORD ABOUT ETYMOLOGY

A word about dolls.

If a doll is a word. And a doll.
If a name, she is, also. Also, and a name. Also, and
a name is a game to play. The word Dolly.

Of the word named "Dolly." *An etymology. Is
derived from. From the British. God or Christian name*, is first.
First her God name, then her father name.
Again, a game! Is etymology. And a story. A story her name is Dolly.

Dolly was a name. *A name for Dorothy.*
Daughter of *England in the 1550s.* Dorothy named of.
God named the father and of England.
And Dorothy. *Dolly – her nickname.* And,

Respectably. Is then my Dorothy. And endearingly. For Dorothy.
Dear Dolly-Dorothy, *interchangeably* –
and yet. *And then a name for his pet, also.* A small animal.
Little animal. Is his. Little pet. *And also named for his mistress.* Dorothy Dolly.
Dolly daughter, Dolly mistress. And still,

Respectably. Is Dolly. If for Dorothy. Or less reputably. If his mistress, less.
Lessly Dorothy, also. Much more Dolly *in the 1640s*, and becoming. Coming.

Dirty. Dirty Dolly. Dirty Dorothy, brittle pet.
Little Dorothy. Be little and still be Dorothy. A little, miss. If not a mistress.
And still becoming. Dirty less.

Less dirty yet. *Circa 1700*, now Doll now Dolly, will she be. Be still
my properly. Dorothy reputably, not less, or yet –
is now a common. A common Dolly. A common Dorothy. *Dolly a first
name* her. A name a God name. Or – also, *just a toy*, a name a game. To play
still a Dolly. Also a Dolly. *A little yet.*

PART FOUR: DOLLY VARDEN AND HER CRUEL LITTLE MUFF

I

Echoing the structure of ancient Egyptian tombs, as well as
more contemporary domestic spaces, the first "Dollhouse"
was commissioned by Albrecht V, Duke of Bavaria in 1558.
He ordered the creation of a miniature palace as a gift for
his small daughter. That she might play with it.

Once completed, he deemed it so magnificent a representation
of the magnificent things that belonged to him that he kept it
for himself. In order. To house his art collection.

First a spectacle of property, the Dollhouse of the Duke became
known as the Munich Baby House and was destroyed in a fire
in 1674. However, a detailed inventory of the house and its
contents survives. His dollhouse contained multitudes, which
included: the three kitchens of the Duke's wife, a wine cellar,
a coach house, parlours, nurseries and on the third floor was
the ballroom.

Also on the premises: a chapel, complete with miniature priest.

II

First created as displays of personal belongings, the dollhouse
became popular in Germany, Holland and England in the 1700s.
Wealthy families would commission its creation, housing mini-
aturized versions of their most cherished and valuable possess-
ions. For exhibition. The early dollhouses could be both closed
and locked.

III

Only much later were dollhouses created for the purpose of play; and, indivisibly, for pedagogical purposes.

Those who could not afford to have one commissioned, either for their possessions or for their children, were instructed to make them by hand.

Popular instructions for homemade dollhouses would simply say: "To make a Doll's House, *begin with a bookcase.*"

In Germany, named the "dockehaus," in Holland "Cabinet Houses," and then the "Nuremberg Houses." Later in England, "Baby Houses." Increasingly these were designed *just for children.*

IV

The invention of childhood,

as an era, as a developmental stage, as heterotopia – all deemed worthy of protection – is sometimes attributed to the Romantic poets, although most often to the Victorians who popularized the miniature dollhouse and also created a market and a genre, for children's literature.

In the miniature dollhouse, teatime, played at with the tiniest of tea sets, was a popular Victorian pastime, and a delightful vehicle through which to furnish young girls with moral instruction.

Rooms within rooms, a play within a play. Dollhouses, within which mothers could show daughters not only how to govern servants, but how to behave, and how not to, in a house.

V

That she might play with it.

VI

Dolly Varden was a minor character in Charles Dickens's Victorian
novel *Barnaby Rudge* (1841). The daughter of the locksmith,
Dolly Varden was famous for her radiance.

Dolly's actual features were in fact never described, however,
her attire, and, emphatically, the atmosphere of her abstract beauty
were regaled,

if not outright worshipped.

Dolly Varden dressed "gaily." *That spectacular hat.*

VII

When published, the novel wasn't widely read, yet the character
Dolly Varden gained the reputation, infamous, a petulant coquette,
in public culture. And bewitching.

Known for her "thousand little coquettish ways" –
despite the fact that Dolly spends at least a third of the novel
sobbing.

VIII

Beloved by her parents, Dolly's father instructed her to never
faint (as did her mother so often). Instead, Dolly must concentrate
herself fully on her future husband's happiness. Her mother scolded
her consistently, for any impertinent independence.

Both Dolly's mother and father prayed to her beauty: that it
would earn her a prosperous marriage.

To protect a daughter above all, from fate, or punishment,
of becoming a spinster.

IX

Among her many suitors, upon discovering Dolly's lack of
interest in him,

one of Dolly's admirers determined that he was thereby
unlovable,

"wretched for life." As a result, he concluded that,
if her indifference was in fact permanent, then

"the only congenial prospect left him, was to go for a soldier
or a sailor, and get some obliging enemy to knock his brains out
as soon as possible."

X

In the little-read novel *Barnaby Rudge*, the beautiful Dolly Varden
perpetually wept in private.

On occasion, fainting. Time after time dodging the "attentions" of
important men when she went out in public, and even when she
remained, as she so often did, in her childhood home. All the while,
her mother would patrol her for rudeness, which included declining
old men's "polite" gropings and kisses.

While idealizing Dolly – our carefree coquette – the world neglected
to acknowledge the fact that on multiple occasions, Dolly Varden
just barely escapes the threat of rape.

On one occasion, her assailant infers that he perceives her beauty
as a species of cruelty,

that part of his pleasure would be to overpower her while
she fought.

That he might belong to it.

XI

In more than one instance, the narrator (who is perhaps a figure
for Dickens himself) colludes in admiring how desirable Dolly is,
specifically, when she is endangered:

*In the meantime, Dolly – beautiful, bewitching, captivating little
Dolly – her hair dishevelled, her dress torn, her dark eyelashes
wet with tears, her bosom heaving – her face, now pale*

*with fear, now crimsoned with indignation – her whole self a
hundred times more beautiful in this heightened aspect ...*

*Poor Dolly! Do what she would, she only looked the better
for it, and tempted them the more.*

XII

*... When her eyes flashed angrily, and her ripe lips slightly
parted, to give her rapid breathing vent, who could resist it? ...*

*What mortal eyes could have avoided wandering to the
delicate bodice, the streaming hair, the neglected dress,*

the perfect abandonment and unconsciousness ...

XIII

... of the blooming little beauty?

Or, similarly, as Simon Tappertit, also enamoured with her
(in spite of what he termed the devious, the frivolous, feminine
nature),

was known to put it: *"Yes,*
beautiful Dolly – charmer – enslaver!"

XIV

What came to be known as the Dolly Varden Style of dress, which
swept through England, its colonies and the US, had first been in
fashion much earlier in France.

In the 1770s, the "Polonaise" Style of women's dress was popularized
and remained fashionable in European courts and among continental
aristocracy for twenty years. Some historians posit that its design bore
some modicum of influence by traditional Polish costumery, however,
most scholars of women's fashion history report that this trend was in
no way connected to the cultures of Poland, beyond the penchant for
adopting foreign names as a form of fascination with, and fetishization
of, the exotic.

This style of dressing women comprised a tightly bodiced overdress,
revealing a decorative underskirt, an aristocratic appropriation of the
"peasant" style of dress. The underskirt was topped with several layers
of outer skirts. It was often worn with a sizable crinoline made of bone
or metal, or some variation of it such as a bustle or what was later termed
a crinolette. The outfit would be topped off with a highly decorated hat
made even more becoming with the addition of bows or cherries, and
trimmed with ribbons.

Some claim that the main source of inspiration for the Polonaise Style of dress was the milkmaid, or shepherdess. If beauty, then.

XV

The milkmaid or the shepherdess. How she would have had to gather and raise her skirts, unwatched, in order to work! Her unwitting "provocations." The "suggestiveness," the "exposure" of her underskirts may have endowed the viewer with a sense of the safely scandalous –

due to the unwitting nature of her captivating revelations – and of having power over exhibition, and over her.

XVI

When *Barnaby Rudge* was published in 1841, its reverent descriptions of Dolly Varden defined neither the period nor the specific design of her infamously captivating attire. However, its illustrator, Hablot K. Browne, created drawings in which Dolly wore the anachronistic and "provocative" Polonaise Style of dress.

Three decades after its publication, an extremely costly portrait of Dolly Varden painted by W.P. Frith garnished a startling sum at auction (1870). In it, Dolly wears the Polonaise. Rebecca N. Mitchell reminds us that the fame attributed to Dolly as an objet d'art, and as obsession, had, by then, been removed from "all historical and literary connections."

XVII

The fame surrounding the auction of the portrait of Dolly Varden inaugurated such fervour! And with that, the introduction of the most becoming Dolly Varden (à la Polonaise) Style of dress.

The wearing of the Dolly Varden Style went from "fad" (which
was both a Victorian word and invention) to "craze," worn first
by aristocratic and middle-class women. Then women from lower
classes became able to make, or even sometimes purchase, the
Dolly Varden Style dress since it was becoming, increasingly,
manufactured from cheaper fabrics made en masse.

XVIII

What controversy. Such a dress!

While ads for its loveliness were ubiquitous in women's
magazines, several men of distinction published commentaries;

such address insisted upon the inappropriateness of the
Dolly Varden Style – and so they argued:

In a world in which women's fashion largely masked bodily
functions, such "eruptions of sexuality" and "the force of emotion" –
imposed or invoked within this Dolly Varden fashion – could
make it such that a respectable woman might not be able to go
about her daily business without "becoming provocative."

A milkmaid or shepherdess would not have been able to work
comfortably or skilfully while wearing it.

XIX

Ushered into public imagination, "Such a dress!" suggested
that one could purchase desirability.

And in this way, one could belong to it.

XX

"The very pink and pattern of good looks," Dolly would show up
"in a smart little cherry-coloured mantle," with a hood drawn
over her head.

Upon the hood she wore "a little straw hat trimmed with cherry-
coloured ribbons," which she wore, quite fancifully, "the merest trifle
on one side," which was apparently just enough

"to make it the wickedest and most provoking head-dress that ever
malicious milliner devised."

Her shoes were said to be "heart-rending." Those cherry-coloured
decorations "brightened her eyes" and "vied with her lips."

And to top it all off, Dolly dared wear

"such a cruel little muff" – what *"wickedness."*

XXI

The most popular mass-produced toys in the Victorian era were
dolls for girls and toy soldiers for boys. The most costly dolls were
dressed in elegant dresses, often identical to those of their owners,
and frequently finished off with fancy hats.

In the early to mid-1800s, tiny porcelain dolls fashioned of plain white
bisque were made as single units, without joints. First popularized
in Germany, these tiny nude dolls were made for the bath,

and for placing in cakes.

During the Victorian era, these miniature dolls became known as Penny Dolls due to their new affordability and were sold in the millions.

After the 1850s, Penny Dolls slowly began to be known by a new name: Frozen Charlotte Dolls, first in the US, after the publication of a poem by journalist Seba Smith in 1843. The poem "A Corpse Going to a Ball" was ostensibly based on a true account published in a New York daily in 1840, and was turned into a ballad well-known across the US, in Western Canada and later in England.

In both poem and the later ballad, Little Charlotte.

Little Charlotte who removed her overcoat on a carriage ride to show off her beauty. Then Little Charlotte, she then froze to death.

A jaunty popular cautionary tale to denounce feminine vanity, a common theme among ballads that typically chronicled plots of violence against women and girls, committed whether they "misbehaved," or not.

Frozen Charlotte Dolls, wildly popular in the US and Britain, and recently discovered at an archaeological dig in New Zealand that dates back to the 1800s, were sometimes also accessorized,

and sold with tiny coffins.

XXII

As an extension of the short-lived Dolly Varden Style fad in women's fashion, it followed that *the very name Dolly Varden* – further removed from the novel's actual coquette, and from the style of dress – was disseminated further still throughout British colonies.

In name alone: Dolly Varden became the signifier for beauty itself.

XXIII

Then came innumerable commercial products *bearing her name!*

Many of which were mass-produced and distributed across English
colonies and in the US:

The Dolly Varden Cough Elixir, the horseshoe, the dog collar
and the men's razor strops.

The name "Dolly Varden" crowned a mountain range in Nevada,
a diamond mine in British Columbia and several baseball teams
throughout the US in the nineteenth century. Teams were
owned by males and comprised mostly male players, except
for the all-female African American team from Chester, Pennsylvania,
owned and assembled by a barber turned entrepreneur.

In the US, a discrete *trout* fish, *Salvelinus malma*, was named also
after "her." He dresses in grey where he can be seen, elsewhere,
underneath, he shimmers pinkish and green. The Dolly Varden crab,
Hepatus epheliticus, still travels in the Atlantic, from the US to
the Dominican Republic. Reclusive, flagrant with unabashed spots.

In both England and its colony New Zealand, recipes still teach us
how to bake a Dolly Varden cake. A layered cake topped with edible
flowers, a "highly geological, homemade cake," blushing with
green icing and pink spots, akin to a sneaky trout.

Scholars of Desserts believe this was the precursor to the modern
"Barbie Cake" in which the doll is inserted – half in, half out –
once baked.

XXIV

In the end of the novel *Barnaby Rudge*, Dolly Varden's reputation
is salvaged through marriage. Dolly is admired for adopting docility
and proudly bears many rosy children for her beloved husband,

to whom her devotion is bound by death.

XXV

Most beguiling among objects named after Dolly Varden was the
Dolly Varden Crinoline Lady Tea Service: a full porcelain tea set
manufactured in England from 1927 until the late 1930s.

To this day, Dolly Vardens silent sit and sit upon it.

XXVI

The hand-painted illustrations of Dolly Varden on the art deco
"Crinoline Lady" tea set bear uncanny resemblance to drawings
in Victorian children's books,

stropped with flagrant roiling smocks and wayward hats,
and, notably,

the hand-painted Dolly Vardens resemble the ludic, "child-like"
illustrations by that selfsame era poetess christened Florence Margaret,
who, born on the hem of the Victorian era (1902), published during the
time of the tea set's production

under the self-fashioned nom de plume *Stevie Smith*.

XXVII

In her poem "I Hate this Girl,"
Stevie Smith introduces us to the dilemma of a male narrator
who, finding that the girl he so desires has no interest in returning
his affections, then deems her "cold."

He confesses that while he should very much like to kill her,
what he does instead is to kiss her and kiss her, while wishing
that she might kiss him too.

XXVIII

Most peculiar among domestic objects for sale bearing Dolly Varden's
name was a series of eponymous metallic coffins.

PART FIVE: "GOD IS MAN'S DOLL, YOU ASS!"

I

Neighbourhood children thought that British "poetess" Stevie Smith
was in fact a witch.

II

"So I wear a tall hat on the back of my head that is rather a temple
And I walk rather queerly and comb my long hair
And people say, Don't bother about her,"
states the female narrator in Stevie's poem "Magna Est Veritas."

III

After her father deserted her family when she was three, Florence
Margaret, nicknamed Peggy, lived with her mother and sisters in
North London. When her mother became ill, her spinster aunt Madge
Spear, the "Lion Aunt," came to live with them. Her mother died
when Peggy was sixteen.

Soon afterwards, in the 1920s, Peggy started writing with more
concentration.

It was around this time that she began to call herself Stevie, after a
friend offered the complicated observation that Peggy resembled a
jockey of the same name. At first apprehensive about this new masculine
or androgynous nickname, she went on to adopt this moniker.
For her writing.

Stevie, her sisters and her spinster aunt continued to reside there
after the death of Stevie's mother, Ethel.

"It was a house of female habitation,
Two ladies fair inhabited the house,
And they were brave. For although Fear knocked loud
Upon the door, and said he must come in,
They did not let him in."

A wearer of hats deemed "eccentric," at times, even "inappropriate,"
dressed famously in that starched white Peter Pan collar. Her pale
white skin. Stevie lived out the rest of her days in that house
"of female habitation."

IV

The Dolly Varden Crinoline Lady Tea Set (pattern number 739443
registered in 1928) included teacups and saucers, a small jug for
cream and a bowl for sugar, modest-sized plates, a separate
platter for cakes, a single vase and, of course, a teapot.

All items belonging to the tea service were made of Melba Bone China
(the trade name used by Mayer & Sherratt, which was forced to
restrict production and closed in 1941 under the Wartime Concen-
tration Scheme. It was later reopened as Melba China Co. Ltd. and
closed shop permanently in 1951). The Wartime Concentration
Scheme banned the production of hand-painted or "decorated"
china, deeming beautiful things to be "frivolities" that prevented
workers from producing pragmatic objects, or from attending to more
productive contributions to the domestic War Effort.

A variation of a reproduction of a reproduction of Dolly Varden
bedecked in her famous "provoking" hat, endless scarf and infinite
crinoline is hand-painted onto every object in the tea set. Upon all
its out-turned surfaces bright pastel colours – periwinkle, lavender,
pistachio, buttercup – and the most fanciful swooshing linework.

Her variations.

V

Stevie Smith's writing career coincided with a post-Victorian
backlash against the "gallant wartime gals" who, either out of
necessity or inclination, or both, refused the pressure to return
to domesticity after World War I. Working as a secretary, Stevie
would wile away angular boredom by writing novels, and later,
poems on yellow legal pads, waiting for the hired girl to trundle
in with the tea trolley.

Such working women were dubbed deviants in the 1920s and '30s:

"hussies, pin-money girls, dole-scroungers" who stole the
jobs of men, and were said to deserve the punishment of
spinsterhood.

VI

Dolly Varden turns to stare at us. From the centre, or nearly, of
this teacup, from this small round-edged square plate for cakes.
In fact, her face is not quite centred, *more so – it's her hat.*
You see, she had to turn, aslant, to look at me.

Otherwise, she's leaning to our left. Her hat gapes, its outer lip
is foghorn-shaped. It looks a bit like a bib for the mind. Its system
points outwards and away, as if extending, offstage might have been
her gaze. She is unsmiling. The background is white; her portrait,
without context or relation. We see her here, exhibited, but only half.
The rest of Dolly cut off at her midriff.

VII

Below her midriff, her tight turquoise bodice pinches at the middle.
Then it inflates into such preposterous voluptuous chartreuse crino-
lines five times her width. And with her hand she steadies that small
pot of blooms perched oddly atop her skirts mellifluous and roiling
into which she sinks or drowns which. She must keep still or it will
pitch. Three flowers bloom among themselves but a single one
droops in which.

VIII

The Dolly Varden Crinoline Lady Tea Set was mass-produced in the late
1920s and 1930s' interwar era in England. Therein, many held the belief,
inherited from the Victorian era, that men and women belonged,
by nature, to formalized respective spheres, public and private. Many
directed women who had worked in public during World War I to return to
work in the home, or sought to mobilize and control women who remained
workers in public.

Tea sets were prized as utilitarian "domestic" objects and were also
cherished as monuments of civility, emblematic of both status and
morality. Some cost such a pretty penny.

The ubiquitous social ritual of "teatime," a performance of civility,
was popularized in England first among aristocrats. It had already
become fashionable in Europe, and was introduced to British royalty
through the tastes of Catherine of Braganza of Portugal, Bride of
Charles the Second. She was, for a time, Queen of England, Scotland
and Ireland. When she first arrived in England, she was mocked.
For being "so unfashionable!"

Queen Catherine served tea in her wedding to the King in 1662.
Thereby, she introduced this product and ritual, which boasted properties
medicinal. At the time, tea was costly, a signifier of wealth. It became

more popular among all classes once it became cheaper, and when sweetened with sugar.

The consumption of tea, with or without sugar, became an effective way to maintain the energy levels of factory workers who were often overworked and undernourished.

Tea was first imported from China, as was the art of making delicate porcelain, in Britain,

for purposes such as the making of dolls. And tea sets.

IX

At one time England's most famous female poet, Stevie Smith
is best known for her short rhyming poem in which a sinking figure
is memorialized through its titular line, "Not Waving but Drowning,"
published a few months before her rumoured, and failed, suicide
attempt.

Stevie began her long career as a secretary for a publisher of
women's magazines at the age of eighteen, an industry that
she in fact despised; at the same time that she applied herself
to her writing.

She remained part of the workforce, and a publishing writer, for
most of her lifetime.

X

During this interwar era, British factories often separated male and
female workers. Many factories in England had begun to mass-produce
"homely" or "homelike" utilitarian domestic objects for female
consumers, with the additional purpose of beautifying the domicile.

Some termed this the "domestication" of factories wherein factories reproduced idealizations of female domesticity, and then extended this to the state.

Some factories began to enforce *"Visits"* by female Inspectors, both within working hours, and even conducting mandatory home visits to female workers during off-hours.

To enforce the moral propriety of working women.

XI

On every saucer, teacup and each plate, vermilion or sapphire, Dolly's scarf flaps. Away – and waving, flag-like, then flies off. It is exceeding her – but then turns back –

her scarf appears again, at the same time, along the outskirts of each cup and plate, in duplicate. It replicates enforcing bright the border of each teacup rim, the frame of every modest-sized white plate.

If you look back where she's not quite centred – her face at first a girl's but then perhaps also a boy's beguiles and which is which upon your plate. *Your cream tart it will cover her whole face.*

XII

Some contemporary factory owners engaged the Victorian belief in the power of art,

and with genuine concern for how decor might affect the "delicate natures" of their female workers, many began to put in effort to spruce up factory decor, while making no changes to divisions of labour, work and safety conditions, nor to the radical discrepancies between the wages of male and female workers. Women were generally paid one-third of Men's Wage.

At the time, England was a major manufacturer of china, also named porcelain. Working conditions in the porcelain industry were harsh, involving long hours, a lack of sanitation, extended exposures to dusts and toxic paints in cramped, poorly ventilated quarters.

Circa 1870, painting had become an acceptable hobby for monied women of England and women within its colonies since it was presumed that women had little else to do "other than to read novels" while the men of the households were away at business.

Women and girls were often segregated, apart from men, in Workshops wherein, over and over, they hand-painted near-identical images on countless beautiful white china teacups and plates.

Female factory workers who hand-painted porcelain were named "decorators," *emphatically not artists.*

XIII

Circa late 1920s until well into the 1950s in England and the US, advertisers began to incorporate attributes derived from avant-garde European art, which erupted circa 1907 to around 1923.

Challenges to traditional representation introduced by avant-garde painting, sculpture and writing such as Cubism and Surrealism –

non-linearity, fragmentation and multiplicity, the uncanny divorce of subject from a naturalized setting or background –

were appropriated for advertising purposes.

This aesthetic strategy was intended to connote an era of forward-thinking progress to consumer markets. Consumer markets were comprised, increasingly, of large numbers of women;

advertising for female shoppers often conflated images of white female celebrities, aesthetics derived from women's fashion magazines and fashion photography. Ads for female buyers often vacillated between representations of idealized domesticity and moderate freedoms for married, and later unattached (at least in the freedom of the frame of the ads), women. Delightful lifestyles which could be acquired, as the ads suggested, through fashion and consumerism.

Women were increasingly purchasing clothing, "Domestic Items" such as household appliances and prepared or preservable

"Foodstuffs."

XIV

In her small, two-lined poem "The Small Lady,"
Stevie speaks of The Small Lady who resides within her
"beautiful dream," in front of her sizable, "mighty"
washing machine.

XV

Apart from Victorian novelist Charles Dickens's infamous protagonist Miss Havisham, Stevie Smith – *who at times referred to her poems as her children* – was English literature's most famous spinster.

XVI

Prized for its high levels of "whiteness" and "translucency," Bone
China derives its name from the bone ash of animals that comprises
part of its base elements. Animal by-products for England's bone china
industry were sourced from local slaughterhouses and cattle markets,
which were often located within the same districts as porcelain manu-
facturers.

Created from a soft paste made with calcined animal bones, mostly
cattle, this paste was then mixed with clay and stone. White firing
clay was mixed with glassy frit; frit is a flux and it causes pieces to
vitrify when fired in a kiln.

Once fired, the "body" of porcelain would then be converted to a
hard bisque or *bisquit*, as were dolls at the time.

The bisquit would then be glazed twice or thrice. The underglaze,
glaze and overglaze can easily be compared to the layering

of corsets or cakes.

XVII

Stevie's rhyming verse was replete with her illustrations similar
to the drawings included with Edward Lear's literary nonsense
verses (published in 1846),

and also similar to
illustrations in Victorian children's books.

Her verses were frequently praised for their "simplicity."
Just as often, her body of work, both her rhymes and visual art,
were dismissed as eccentric, infantilized as "innocent" and
miniaturized to the status of "decorative."

(Her grandfather, too, used to make fun of her mother, for the simple, "sentimental nature" of her paintings.)

Stevie, who grappled with clinical depression, either throughout her lifetime or intermittently, was widely considered a poetess *"of light-hearted verse"*;

light-hearted themes, which concerned her deeply, if implicitly, if wryly, *throughout her body of work* included her "Servant" death/ Death, economic injustice and the violent eviction of women from our problematized bodies.

And of course, she toyed, ever playfully,
with the light-hearted subject of millinery.

XVIII

Porcelain "bodies" would then either be illustrated with the use of a stencil, or expert hand-painters could paint directly upon the bodies with fine brushes. Paints were often made of toxic metal oxides and all processes sputtered with incredible volumes of dusts.

Female factory workers would walk to and from work through streets and alleys seeping with runoff from the slaughterhouses, from whence came the materials required for their craft. They would step daintily through refuse and offal and such wet, splash- ing mucks. Women's moral fortitude and reputations were deter- mined by their comportment, and the absence of disreputable soilings anywhere upon the body, bodice or hems of their floor- length, at times en-crinolined, multilayered dresses.

XIX

Stevie created and published numerous drawings to accompany
or, conceivably, *as part of* her rhyming verse.

Among them, her often fainting, frowning and fleeing women
were frequently dressed to the nines,

> *and were, so emphatically, doll-like.*

(*What lively baroque chapeaux stropped with baubles! What
voluminous enfrockmentery! What illustrious dresses, cascadinous
tresses.*)

Within her illustrated depictions of husbands and wives,
oftentimes, the only figure represented with any measure of whimsy
or mobility was –

(and gesticulating towards the outskirts of the page) –

That woman's hat!

XX

Women and girls who painted porcelain in factories were known
to give off at all times the unfeminine scent of turpentine;

"paintresses" was the "quaint" term for girls and women who
painted innumerable reproductions in deplorable conditions,

and, considered mere "amateurs," *they were never permitted
to sign their names to their work.*

XXI

In her poem "The Hat," one of several on the subject of women and millinery fashion, Stevie includes an illustration, one among innumerable, in which a dejected-looking woman is crowned with an exuberant, outward-reaching hat.

In its sparse four lines, the poem presents its first-person narrator who loves her hat "more than anything." She appears convinced that it will generate a "wedding ring."

The narrator looks forward to her future wedding with the king who will make her "his own." As a wife, she will keep herself busy by walking "on the palace wall."

In its intertextual sister-poem, living right next door on the next page, Stevie's poem "Thank You" embodies a continuation of the poem "The Hat" in both its versification and its illustration.

Therein, two girls or young women, orphaned siblings with odd, somewhat androgynous faces,
peer down, or out, over what appears to be a ledge, rooftop or palace wall:

"What are we looking for over the wall?

We are not looking for anything at all."

XXII

*No records of the name of the artist who created the design
for the first Dolly Varden Crinoline Lady,* whom women and girls
then hand-painted and painted on innumerable Crinoline Lady
Tea Set parts – the designer most likely a woman or a girl –
have been preserved.

XXIII

As it happens, one of the earliest poems, if not the earliest written by Stevie in her youth, tells the story of a sister. Finding that her only or best method to retaliate against her brother who has insulted her (with a slur combining misogyny and racism in which he sexualizes and demonizes her beauty mark)

is to launch her beloved hat right at him!

XXIV

When Stevie began writing more seriously, representations of independent women in women's magazines typically re-incorporated women into "respectability" through marriage; or misbehaving and unmarried women were frequently, finally, killed off in plots.

Stevie was "scrupulously suspicious" of romantic colonial fiction propagated for women by commercial ventures, by artists and by the state. Such narratives, she believed, fostered female dependency.

When Stevie began writing (1920s) and then publishing (1930s), England considered itself teeming with what were termed "superfluous" unmarried women.

XXV

One of the, if not the only, instances in which Stevie Smith chose to include an illustration of women partaking in the ubiquitous British ritual of "teatime" takes place in the poem entitled "The Broken Friendship."

While many of Stevie's poems focus on the mental and physical conditions of women and girls whose lives are mediated by males, this poem focuses specifically on unmediated female inter-relations.

The poem tells the story of Easter Ross and Jolie Bear (whose names are rather curious – "E. Ross" and her beautiful, animal-like companion). In the related illustration, the pair sit at tea in a living room or parlour, drawn with surreal, disjunctive proportions and furnishings.

Easter tells Jolie that her heart is broken;
Jolie Bear says nothing. She passes a plate
"as if she had not heard."

It follows that Mrs. Easter Ross takes to her bed, wishing for, or anticipating, only death. Mrs. E. Ross seems comforted only by the hope that pretty Jolie Bear shall "carry the harrow" at her funeral.

The drawing of the two female friends at tea is bizarre, to the point of jarring. The proportions of the room are chaotic, queer, irregular; the women, rather androgynous.

On our right, a woman we may presume is Jolie, since she seems to be the listener, watches her friend from under the brim of her emphatically conservative flat hat.

On our left, the woman with her mouth open as if speaking must be Easter Ross. E. Ross holds the teapot. Its upward-pointing spout points in the direction of Jolie. Both E. Ross and her armchair are disproportionately tall. Her head in fact exceeds the height of the curtain rods on the wall.

Between them, a table set for tea. Each, in her armchair, separately.

(*"Everything went out of her | When Jolie never spoke."*)

Behind Jolie, a bookcase. And a tall lamp weeping tassels, which
trail downward from its long, stringed, flaccid switch.

XXVI

Stevie Smith's illustrations for her poems bear influence from
avant-garde European art, which posed a challenge to conventional
mores by disrupting our ways of seeing.

Stevie's drawings mime traditionalism, then disrupt it through
flourishes of derangement, disproportion, fragmentation –
what nonsense.

A similar palette of avant-garde aesthetics was appropriated for
marketing purposes during Stevie's lifetime. However, their aim
differed from that of Stevie. Advertisers, aiming to sell as many
products as possible, rebranded domesticity as a strategy to
continue to sell it to women and to men.

The Dolly Varden Crinoline Lady Tea Set also bears the influence
of avant-garde aesthetic traditions. Whether out of deference,
or resistance, Dolly maintains her silence. As to which.

XXVII

In 2023, the National Poetry Library in London, England, presented the
exhibit named *Poets in Vogue* in which actual clothes worn by poets,
as well as artistic impressions of famous outfits, were placed on display.

Purportedly a feminist show, only famous clothes of famous female poets
were exhibited.

The show included the plaid skirt Sylvia Plath wore to Paris in 1956.
Also, rhymestress Edith Sitwell's floor-to-ceiling gown worn when
she performed as Lady Macbeth. The asymmetrical caftan worn by Audre
Lorde after her mastectomy. And stencilled on fabric, a figure holding
the words from Theresa Hak Kyung Cha's famous performance: "Me,"
"Fail," "Words." Another exhibit bore the garments Theresa wore when
she was raped and murdered in New York City in 1982 at the age of
thirty-one.

For Stevie Smith, an exhibit of rows upon rows of starched white Peter
Pan collars, which, some suggested, was to connote her aesthetic
investment in repetition. (*Her variations.*)

XXVIII

In Stevie's poem "The Sad Heart," the female narrator expresses her
dejection.

That perhaps she should not, does not deserve – to "be" –
since she had been spared: *from beauty.*

The omniscient narrator in Stevie's poem entitled "Pretty" regales
instances of prettiness in nature, particularly among predators,
especially animals that stalk other animals, and it offers the admonition
that were one to cry out, "pretty," repeatedly, "pretty, pretty, pretty"
then:

"... you'll be able
Very soon not even to cry pretty
And so be delivered entirely from humanity
This is prettiest of all, it is very pretty."

XXIX

Regularly, repeatedly, the women and girls in Stevie Smith's
illustrations can only imagine escape to move livable
circumstances:

through art or through death.

The illustration for the poem entitled "Pretty." That calm-faced girl
or woman who sits and sits quietly upon a chair underneath a
fantastic, animated hat.

A dead pussy reclines in her lap.

XXX

Stevie was to be handed the Gold Medal for Poetry from the
hand of the Queen of England in 1969. Journalists were aflutter
with accounts of Stevie's attire, and quoted the vicar who stated
that:

"Everybody thought it was   killingly
funny that that hat
was going up to the Queen."

Stevie is rumoured to have selected a hat for her appearance at
Buckingham Palace from a second-hand jumble sale.

She was, as they believed, "fully aware" of what one
should wear – and not –
to be seen

by the Queen.

None had, as of yet, taken seriously Stevie's careful studies of women's millinery. Hence, none bothered to document or study the attributes of that particular hat. Never for a moment giving her credit for that. *For that hat, as an act, of ekphrasis.*

PART SIX: BEWARE OF DOMESTIC OBJECTS

Meeting on a young girl's breast. Or a cream tart ...
(as spoken by P. in dialogue with E. in "Exercise on Two Notes")
    CLAUDE CAHUN, Trans. Susan de Muth

I

"An idea which undresses itself. I guarantee it.

It was delivered to
me naked.

I am only responsible for the swimming costume ..."

wrote Claude Cahun in her poem, or "'Letter to the Chief
of Police, the district' Paris, 25 April, 1925."

II

Born in France and self-named at the age of twenty, at
eighteen, artist and activist Claude Cahun (née Lucy Renee
Mathilde Schwob) began taking self-portraits most
provocative.

Loosely affiliated with Surrealist artists of her time, Claude's
performances, collages, hybrid writings and self-portraits were
largely disregarded by better-known male artists.

Within at least one self-portrait she poses *as a doll*.

III

Ekphrasis: Claude leans to the right, which is your left in the old
black and white photograph. Her chemise, from abdomen to the
top of her chest, held together with black sutures. The letter X.
Her arms held behind her back, her pose highly unnatural, doll-like.
For staring back, her stolid gaze composed. Piled or tied around
her head that braid of cloth "looks just like bread."

IV

Claude Cahun's photographic self-portraits taken in the late 1920s
and 1930s mimicked, after a fashion, women's fashion magazines
and ads for all manner of:

Domestic Objects, women's clothing and accessories,
and Foodstuffs.

Having originated when clothing designers moved from using
living female "mannequins" hired to be still to the use of anonymous,
sometimes-moving female models, fashion photographs first served
the purpose of creating records to prove ownership of his designs.
And then he would sign his name upon them.

Claude posed, then photographed, her self or their selves in various
guises, modelling the various identities available for women, albeit
some of said portraits were rather anomalous.

The multiple staged female selves of her photos were rendered
identifiable by what each of her wore, and where each of her
was housed.

V

Among her numerous self-portraits, Claude refused to identify if,
which, of her self was the original.

Clad often with head shaved, at other times masquerading
in hats, costumes, then parading the regalia – of "women,"
of "men," of both, of neither and, in one beguiling photo,

as one who reclines in a fork drawer.

VI

I began to fall in love with her variations.

VII

In 1936, Claude Cahun contributed an essay, "Beware of Domestic
Objects," a leftist-inflected manifesto, along with a sculpture
fashioned from found domestic objects, to an exhibition of
contemporary Surrealist art. In her manifesto, the insistence that
the menace of domestic objects lies in their polysemous natures:
they double as objects most utilitarian, also serve as
instruments *for the purpose of play. And in this they become
dangerous.*

The exhibition included the famous *Une Tasse En Fourrure,*
or *Le Déjeuner en Fourrure* (*Breakfast in Fur*) by Meret
Oppenheim, a sculpture in which Meret exhibited an unremarkable,
ubiquitous, household teacup and saucer. Each of its supple concave
surfaces was enwrapped in a sumptuous pelt of fur, and the fur-covered
spoon that ran away with the dish appears as if it is sinking within it.

VIII

Sometime in the 1920s, Lotte Pritzel was commissioned, by a German
manufacturer, to incorporate her Wax Dolls in advertisements
for biscuits.

IX

Claude Cahun and lifetime partner Marcel Moore (née
Suzanne Alberte Malherbe), both artists and cross-dressers,
created the name "The Soldier Without a Name"

then signed this name to anti-Nazi leaflets they wrote and dispersed
in secret to the families of German soldiers. Through the imagined
body of a male soldier, they impersonated the personification of
resistance.

Their flyers were composed of Nazi slogans rearranged and
disarticulated, reduced to infantile jingles. In the style of avant-
gardist collage. Their anti-propaganda art comprised fragmented
deconstructions of the bodies of dismantled Nazi propaganda
speeches. The flyers were sometimes illustrated

with child-like drawings.

X

In one remaining illustrated flyer created by either, or the
pair, Claude and Marcel, the hand-drawn picture resembles
the drawings in children's books.

In it, a small sailor man flails in his sinking boat although it
has not yet capsized.

Alone in his small ship, half of which is submerged, he waves
as the flag of his ship (that bears a swastika) trails off outside the
frame, its rivulets shapely as a woman's scarf, which performs a
visual echo, in variation, of the tumult of the waves below.

All the while the heads of a pair of fishes –
just barely visible above the surface of water –

look on and on.

XI

In infantile scrawl, the illustration's child-like rhyming poem,
akin to a limerick, goes something like this:

I believe the waves devoured
In the end, both boatman and boat.
And this, on behalf of his roar.
And now ... Adolf Hitler is a goner!

It has been signed "Colonel Heine."

XII

Flyers such as this, in the dead of night, clandestinely inserted
into mailboxes, on car windshields.

XIII

Their parodic limerick is a play on the famous poem "Die
Lorelei" by German poet Heinrich Heine, which had also been
set to music by composers such as Franz Liszt. Heine's work was
said to have become increasingly parodic.

The original poem was based on a German legend in which
one or several mermaids or women are blamed for causing
the deaths of men at sea:

they must have distracted them with their beauty.

In Claude and Marcel's version, the man waving, near-drowning
in his ship is a figure for Hitler as well as for the nation itself,
signified metonymically by the sinking ship bearing the name
Das Reich, the Realm.

XIV

In the early 1920s, German-born immigrant Baroness Elsa von Freytag-
Loringhoven would stroll down the streets of Greenwich Village
in New York, performing her "Art Walks" about town, adorned in
a homemade costume consisting of multiple odds and ends,
Domestic Objects and toys.

Prior to working as an artist, she had worked as an artist's model,
a shop window mannequin, a wife and a prostitute.

The Art Walks of Baroness Elsa. Her head shaved, she would paint
her face, on occasion, vermilion, attaching postage stamps to it.
Her lipstick, black. Her vestments and accoutrements fashioned from
found, sometimes stolen (she did several stints in jail for theft),
materials.

Among objects with which she adorned herself:

"a burnished coal scuttle for a helmet strapped to her head with a
scarlet belt which buckled under the chin, Christmas tree balls of yellow
and red as ear rings, a tea strainer about her neck, a short yellow skirt
barely covering her legs, and over the precision of her breasts a single
length of black lace she would walk the city,"
wrote Djuna Barnes in 1933.

Also:
a string of dried figs, mustard spoons, a birdcage inhabited by a
dejected canary, tin cans, cutlery, pilfered curtain rings. On more
than one occasion she was seen wearing a tomato can bra on blue string.

Moreover, *the hats!*
Sometimes made with carrots and beets. At times she also sported a
plaster phallus; other times she carried just a rat.

Caroline Knighton notes that the Baroness was as if "cast"
as some form of "midtown Medusa."

XV

Stevie Smith, autodidact and rhymestress, read widely among
historical and modernist works, including avant-garde poetry.
One of the first readers of the poems of her youth pronounced
them "unnecessary"; the first reader of her first novel judged it
to be spirited, yet perverse, conceding to the possibility that it
might contain some other thing. Which as her first reader, she
may very well have missed. Stevie once wrote: "Me for Dada."

XVI

How the Baroness insisted,

that a woman's aging body is not an object of shame.

And she frequently (while borrowing money to live from most
everyone she knew) bemoaned the fact that no one would pay
her for her Dada art walks.

Jane Heap, the publisher of *The Little Review*, a vital repository
of progressive and banned works of its time, once described the
Baroness as she who "dresses dada, loves dada, lives dada."

Art historians often now call her its mother. Mother of Dada.

The Baroness also decorated herself *with toys* – mainly toy soldiers –

the name
given to the dolls made just "for boys."

XVII

Before taking her life at the age of fifty-three, on her fiftieth birthday,
the Baroness made her appearance at the French consulate:

wearing hip-length rubber boots, a ballet skirt made of paper and fifty
candles lit,

on the real birthday cake she wore as a hat.

XVIII

Engendering controversy, cross-dressing artists Claude Cahun
and her or their lover Marcel were sentenced to death for the
creation of art deemed "degenerate."

XIX

"I slip on female duds and my Dolly Varden," said Lieutenant
Commander Scobie on one of his long walks through the Arab quarter
in the city of Alexandria, Egypt, during wartime in the 1930s.

There, he believed, he would be safer; since he was a police officer.
If ever questioned he could say he was simply in disguise,

but never wanton.

And wearing such a conspicuous hat, and flapping scarf, and that women's dress in Lawrence Durrell's novel *Justine*, Lieutenant Scobie's life was taken at the hands of British soldiers from Her Majesty's Ship *Milton*.

PART SEVEN: THE CRINOLINE LADY
NOTES ON EKPHRASIS

for HETTE

Yet cognitively the dollhouse is **gigantic.**
> Susan Stewart, *On Longing: Narratives of the Miniature, the Gigantic, the Souvenir, the Collection*

I

Dolly Varden Crinoline Lady Tea Set, circa 1930.

Orphan parts purchased: three saucers, two teacups, one tiny two-tiered stand for tiny cakes.

Purchased and shipped to Canada from Mother England, 2021.

While this particular cup and saucer have been painted with precision, this singular pair has, *scandalously, been signed*; each object bears, on its underside, this hand-painted signature that resembles the writing of a child, by:

"HETTE."

II

Whatever it was I was searching for, website after website, by some mad accident I was

confronted by *The Crinoline Lady.*

The sight of her, some instant recognition. Which, as you will discover, becomes more and more rare the longer we live. Harrowing.

I had to buy her so I could look and look.

III

Look at them. Curios and china cabinets – everywhere, filled with inter-changeable and near-valueless hand-painted porcelain plates and cups and saucers painted by, by now, anonymous (see them) –

ancestresses trying not to go out of their minds.

IV

As it happened, this encounter with the Crinoline Lady transpired during the only time in my adult life in which I could barely imagine living any longer.

V

At night, Dolly and I wander the shelves of our curio wearing our obscene bodies. She prefers to sleep in the corner by the discreetly dissident antique spoon with her rusting neckline. Myself, I press my face to the smudged glass. "I promise."

To help Dolly find where they put the rest of her torso.

"I am practicing kindness."

VI

The Crinoline Lady, Dolly, she must have reminded me of that childhood
tea set given to me when I was too old to play with it as a toy, yet exactly
the right age for an encounter *with art*. That tea set designed for the
purpose of play with the doll and the self. That most nuanced aspect of
play fostered by the imagination: *interpretation*.

An inexpensive miniature tea set with "just that girl" and some flowers
hand-painted on every piece, given by some well-intending relative
who hoped that a child would keep being that wished-for, underestimated
version of a child, not this. This other version of childhood, the child already
aware of expulsion.

Childhood days glimmering prickly and experimental by the black vestibule
cross-legged glamorous unfolding pastries whose inestimable folds suddenly
gush cherries operatic. This fated need for affection among encircling brutish
playmates pre-moral and stinking of hogsugar impossible to distinguish the
sadists from the merely fearful. Apprentices to the fantastic and limits.
Then, narrative.

Hush acrobatic magazines of naked ladies by the creek make our faces
burn for days until we can't remember that feeling just electrify forbidden.
Headiness of belonging. Flâneur of childhood. Powdered milk. The riddle of
confidence. She doesn't make me play outside, that bespectacled babysitter
instead lets me incant silk the big words on bared spines of adult books on her
shelves "*photo.graphy.*" Our absolute keepers who too weep. When walls rumble
money, alcohol, but love. Can you hold it the blueberry between your lips and
not bite it *how long?* Constitutive incompleteness. Always acting out and can
one save one's mother. Then, nothingness. *Wrong again!* This agonized
plenitude. Strange girl patent-leather shoes *but I love the black buckles.*
No proof of their god anywhere.

She was a strange girl. On the tea set of my childhood, oddly proportioned and
alone, standing awkwardly on the miniature cups and plates, among also-
awkward flowers that, stylized in the Romantic tradition, signified futurity while
personifying artifice. The background otherwise blank as if history invisible.

The bodies of flowers, whom I understood, even then, to be propaganda, imposters. Neither begonias nor tulips, they were born to be the idea of flowers, sentries sent to surround and berate her. From gangly stalks, gangly just like she was, their function in the composition was to enforce the boundaries of representation. They would patrol versions of whom she should be. *How rude,* I thought, even then. To conflate begonia and tulip is a species of negation.

The girl's features were borrowed from the features of girls and of boys. Not exactly cheerless, she was wary. Her stare, capacious, sullen, was not unkind. She stared back the same way Dolly Varden is not-smiling on every saucer. As a child, I did not yet have the word for it. If beauty that I could belong to it.

The girl was somehow: philosophical. I loved her instantly for it.

And not exactly without sex, more like in that moment she wanted to be also. Something other. As if for an instant, the thrum of mind with sex as one of its formidable eventual mouths could pause, say, "Not just yet." Or "And." And so, she was

becoming I imagined her infinite understanding of human cruelty. Then her disdain of our rationalizations for it. (Likely, aspects of the genesis of nonsense verse – that traumatic discovery of the radical failure of human rationality, and the impossibility of our accountability unto it. An aesthetic for this.) And, when she spoke, *"Everything we borrow from eternity we have to give back,"* I imagined someone with me in that Final Act and asked her, *"Will you* meet me –

at the Coat Check?"

VII

"To make a Doll's House: begin *with a bookcase*."

VIII

All afternoon, the kind artist has been painting extravagant future hats
for Dolly and I.

Tuesdays (cousins to blueberries), we play a game called Art,
permitted to indulge our preference for it above the company, endangerous,
of others, for one day.

We chase their wide-brimmed shadows past the corners of the plate, looking,

"Over here –" cries Dolly,
trying on her new set of authentic legs.

IX

Avant-garde, aesthetic, tactical, a woman learns to officiate with her mind.

X

Dolly tells me she can hear my mother wandering barefoot through the
neighbourhood fall red fences calling in my childhood cats when night drops
down voice indivisible from being.

XI

In Stevie's poem "My Hat," its female narrator supposes
that her mother would never notice that the (narrator's) hat,
described as possessing unusual agency, has run away with her.

And waving its swan wing, her hat is said
to become her.

XII

Said Dolly: Hette! Hette! I thought to myself, Becoming, I imagine

                            her "Will you help me carry my story?"

Said Ekphrasis: While we waited for love or gods we talked
                            to dolls.

Letter U:
The Understudy
from *The Chronicles of Chloe and Olivia*

Les Demimondaines, Poem V

I

"And *there you be!*"

said Dona Carlota
as she stitched my new bisque feet
in place at the Doll Hospital. "*See?*

Now wasn't that simple."
"I, be" my voice echoes
in a tone Olivia seems to have trouble discerning.

"And we're off!"
says Olivia.
"To the Marketplace."

She was right.
That part didn't hurt a bit.

II

"Ooooh. Now, we're *in a play*,"

exclaimed Olivia as they herded us
squawking through the turnstile. At the Market,
everything we could imagine. "*Everything,*

is existing all at once!"

Olivia helps me tilt my head to the proper angle as the scarf wearing
that squatting woman flutters, slinks beyond us finding its rightful place
within existence.

III. Event Script for Rhinestones

The drawn woman selling rhinestones
leans back indefatigably. "When you wear *these*:

You must feel just like it looks
like it feels when you see someone
see you notice them
wearing these."

IV

"*But
rhinestones aren't really even very shiny,*"

whispers Olivia,
"*and they look kind of sharp ...*"
eyeing them among the other gems
glistening, earnest sunbathers spread across the garbage bag
taped to the car hood.

The woman seems to understand. (Even though
I'm pretty sure she can't
hear Olivia.) "Their gleaming –
it is private," she confides.

"At night,
tiny women in hairnets descend from the valleys
and powder their crevasses with flour."

V

Sizable people everywhere with many things
to do.

"What could they possibly be thinking!"
I asked of Olivia. In rhetorical fashion,

the question closes up its legs and sits like
that bored dancer, the girl in the apricot leotard who is practising,
absent-mindedly posing as a peach
over by the Dutchess of Jam.

"I don't think emeralds have anything to do."
She pauses, considers this further,
"Nor cups.
Nor saucers.

I am not sure yet. About spoons."

Olivia might be right.
I hold her brand-new reusable bags for her.

VI. Mother Goose

Behind the woman who keeps scooping
glass cupfuls into Olivia's satchel,

a conveyor belt escorts chokecherry Palačinke
round and round, above which she has slung upside-down fowl.

The lozenge she sucks and sucks behind her teeth
clicks, the telegraph machine of heuristic beetles.

Then, with that graceful gesture, she wipes her left hand
on a triangle of white cotton,
leaving behind a sleek streak
of fat from feral geese.

Chloe is keeping still.
The Babushka must have taken this for lack
of satiety. She ladles heaps gently upon the mound.

"Matchka,
now do you have enough?"

VII

THEATRE OF THE SELF: "I suppose I shall be a Strawberry again today,"
sighed the Strawberry.

BRIOCHE: "Noiselessly, and looking straight ahead."

VIII

We wore facial expressions,
Olivia and I. Bemusement, inoffensiveness, aghast.
And the one for awaiting absolution.

Aghast was my favourite.
We donned several hats,
both practical and ruthless.

We paraded rapturous, Among.
Umbrellas, cellphones, the perspectives, pig heads.

Then the Giant Begonias rose up and began to obscure
the fluorescent lights.

When Olivia tugs and tugs at the thread
means "Chloe, *I just want*

to go home."

IX. The Nothingness "Our Lemonade Stand"

Walking back was slower
than getting there
because I'm not so good
at it.

There seems to be no use for the abandoned factories,
except to rent them out for ballroom dancing.

At the "Our Lemonade Stand"
(written by hand over the For Sale sign),
"I think that girl thinks we can't see,"
says Olivia.

She means the tall girl with the natural air kicking the small one
under the TV table.

"She must think we're pretty
stupid," I say.
"Or worse," whispers Olivia, "maybe she doesn't even care
that we can see her!"
Then I realize we have no money.
"We have no money."

"That's okay," says the girl
being kicked. "We're just counting the hours ...
until we are *resplendent*."

"Or," the unapproachable girl corrects her,
"until we can buy fruit out of season."

The girl being kicked starts to cackle,
which shocks Olivia, or fills her with giddy delight.

"Well, then –" she cackles some more
which makes her the Cruel Countess
"– then you can have a glass of Nothingness Lemonade!"

...

As we head back,
they're still at it.

"If *you* didn't drink up all our lemonade!"
"If *you* didn't always start up kicking me."

X. Not So Much a Debate as a Discussion

Olivia and I have so much
"To Discuss" now that we're home.

"A First-hand Witnessing of Violence,
for example," she says.

The tapping sound could be "equal parts
branch or animal," forcing its way
through the fissure in the floorboards
of the Lady's Chamber. "Is it possible,"

she offers, "that the tall one just likes it.
I mean, kicking the other one."

In an effort to be charitable –
either to lessen the superiority of our horror,
or maybe just to make us less alone –
I stretch myself towards: the Invention
of Empathy. "Perhaps
kicking her just helps keep
her new legs in place?"

"Oh, Chloe."

I try to remember to always
look for what Olivia is telling me
when she gives me a look. (That one
is, I think, the one
for when she finds it annoying
that I get to appear more philosophical than she,
because I am the one
telling the story.)

Olivia tells me she would like "To swoon,"
"Again!" and "Soon." So I lock the door
and fasten all the latches.   *"So the Violet Sellers can't get in."*

"But what if they can still get in?"

"This way,
at least we'll know:

If they make it into the lobby.
If they make it into the parlour." I nod,
stringing up the barricade
of Chirping Bells.

And if they make it into the mind ... ? cautions the Plum,
ripening to jelly in the heirloom bowl on the Rhinoceros table steadying on all
fours.

Olivia lowers her gaze. It pauses at the fetal footstool on the mannered purple
rug, upon which the Proprietor liked to rest his drink,
while men of intelligence around him discussed matters of importance.

Then the Head made of Bisque scolds, or is it implores, *"No, no, no,
no, no."*

Letter V:
Variorum, the Imperfect Villainelle

Les Demimondaines, Poem VI

They didn't have meds then ... maybe Sylvia Plath would have made it if she had had sisters.
DIANE SEUSS, Interview

Variorum: An edition of an author's works in which the body of the text
is marked by notes from various editors and commentators.

...

Well, who is at fault
that she fell in the well? "Or –
she vaulted herself" in the vault?

That she faltered in fall,
unwell, in the vault, fell.
Well, prey tell – "Could it be her fault?"

"Ran away with the spoon!" "Not our fault."
The Snow Man would have her "Not tell!" ("*Why I want ...*")
somersaulting the summer with salt.

Listen: violins. Silent as salt.
None heard her: a version, a diction – "Can't tell!"
Her sigh lent a dress. "Who could halt –

her!" Old voices, echoes. From the vault
through the cracks! She fell: "Infidel, Mademoiselle –"
("Why?") None beheld her, altered – "What befell –"

in the salt, in the vault, in the ought ("Not!"), in malt.
"Not?" a chosen farewell. She swelled in her eggshell.
Her silent address. A daughter. A lace halter.
"Who?" Could fault all her self.

Letter W:
The Watchers
"In the Aspic Academy ..."

The Watched
pace in
the Aspic.

"We liked
to watch
Them. *There!*"

What trouble!
To jump in
the jelly dome.

But the Watchers
do not
care.

Letter X:
Xenos

Excerpts from
The Handbook: How to Play with Children from Another Species

The attributes of liminality or of liminal personae ("threshold people")
are necessarily ambiguous ... they are betwixt and between.
  Victor Turner, "Liminality and Communitas"

Dramatis Personae, or Biographies:

One is a House of Care	Xenodochium
(*"Come! Strangers, travellers, the poor and the sick!"*)	
One, That Sailing Ship, Three-Masted	Xebec
One Whose Name Begins as Stranger	Xenos
One, How She Brings Forth	Xenia
One is the Distance Between Guest and Host	Xenia

I. The Xenodochium

We dare approach the Xenodochium.
The House Built Just for Guests in the Walled City.

Closer, the muck-kneed girl
who jabs air with her stick edges

the edge of the courtyard.
She runs her other gummy hand

along the velvet rope, which droops
from impartial, silver-faced stanchions.

Go no further, Mother had said.
"*Not a stick* – it's a baton! A broom,

now a staff. For a Ruler of the Ages!"
She leans half her torso over the line, touching

a blue-nailed hand to her invisible crown
for balance. "But, Mummy, my shadow

over the line isn't the same as me
crossing!" *Careful, they're funny over there,*

says the coughing man imperturbably
from the pedestal wheeled in for Occasions.

II. The Xebec Boats

"My mother is a fish."

    Vardaman Bundren, WILLIAM FAULKNER, *As I Lay Dying*

i

Unwitting Emperor of my Childhood, he always knew when the boats were coming. With his back to harbour-facing windows, from that brown plaid armchair, smoking, the moat of cigarette burns in beige carpet around his veined, bluing ankles, somehow, my father could still see the waters behind him.

His gaze would alight on objects buoying across its surface then take them into itself, exceeding them.

The Xebec boats were coming! The earliest sign: first the sails, three per vessel, oncoming upon the undulating surface within which sea and sky become indistinguishable, closer, uncountable faces peering over the ledge at the stare staring at them: "There they are!"

ii

Objects or creatures pierce the surface of sea, sudden, as if sourceless, residing within depressions in its surface and sealing them shut, becoming part of surface, and bobbing upon it, within it, like cardboard puppets in the hands of the child making them dance this deranged caricature of dancing. Objects entering the mind of water are received. Taken into itself and then exceeding them. Its forehead inscrutable and so vast that pattern becomes inconceivable. Self-referential or without self, the gravity of water. And carries whatever is on it. In it.

As if nostalgic, gravid, the mass of water encircles its containment. Appearing without referent, roiling, near-contempt of its self-reverence. With or without memory. And surges, recovers form, a habit given shape by the shapes of others.

And presses against the boundary of other and raises the question, will it give. Salvaging motion, mindless, pre-barbaric, before logos its lidless looking is not unified and streams. And clapped back shut, it degrades into riddle, reflecting, infinitesimal shatterment of shards of sun.

Even sun must wince, and cannot contain its retort at the sight of its reflection engraved upon water that receives and declines it. Its radiance now summarized, condensed and shattered into stinging spearheads of inter-refractive glimmer, deformed. And forming, the plated plane of the sea puckers, pleats and culls crests, and cinches, accumulating. Fins or blades swell and cloy, now foam-gilded, talons ladle and claw, then topple backward-looking and latch, wilting to rejoin larger, or origin. And pulled to shore across a thinning sheet.

And pulled to shore, a thinning sheet, now a pant leg, spills its cuff of water. And it offers changing objects. Damaged tassels of foam disperse as disparate, yet join. A procession of objects amassed, swaddled, meringue tide is a story: acrobatic wrappers, beaded belts of algae, contorted containers that once contained diapers, soggy dolls lifelike. Archive; which began and which recedes in motion and murmur, plaintive and covetous, suckling outwards from the impetus of hollow, of motion within the shape once forged from ancient speech, the before speech, primordial parent wordless, where memory-making of every transient thing hibernates in its forming.
What could be a tenderness.

iii

Beyond metaphor the waters, sublime, paternal, became a looking glass.
Or an offering. An epistemological structure from which to look upon the world. And offering relation, metonymic, relation of anguish translated as lack which must be, in origin, mine. And from which to marvel at the far shimmer of others. Would that a version of lack could become, instead, inquiry. This would be a gift. To reach him we had to cross water.

Some crossed. Disembarked from the Xebec boats, they assemble and face me. Mirroring my gestures, laying out wares to trade between us across the caking sand. On the shoreline that water tatters, we lay out our wares and daughters in rows. We display notebooks fashioned from necklines of arboretums, stoppered bottles of ink made from the slow body of a fish whose blood is mostly water.

One looks out at me. As he runs his likeable fingers over a homunculus made of sugar his fingernails rest so squarely in the bed of every fingertip, small pillows. Each object he offers retracts its alterity. An object is an object. Then imagination enters, intimate, form-light glints off of it and travels elsewhere, or oblivion, where everything is still possible, *Stranger.*

iv

And so, translation begins as desire begins,
from that place first wordless, and seeking form. She held the phone to his ear
his ear in his hospital bed so that across the distance of three provinces I could
imagine, for him, the least useless words he could take with him.

The last words he spoke fatherly were part fish. *And he became a merman.*

v

The languid tail of water did not flinch. Nor did it acknowledge the ashes of
the man who once showed me how to tame the infuriating curls that I inherited
from him, by passing a man's black plastic pocket comb over them, drenched in
water. And he became the strangest sand I poured beside my brother. Jostled,
thick ash into the river's body, the mind of it, returning to where his favourite
river and horizon might, pre-intimate, a condition of relation to other, indivisible.

And leans away, the water. In its damaged rendition of the masculine, a hand-
me-down force obdurate in reticence, enigmatically solitary. Dogmatic, sublimity
of directionless. At times anachronistic, angry, its privacy just kept. Disconnected
and rehearsing elegy, and so secretly fragile. Ritualized and shivering in

victorious sad detachment. The pomp of a general's tent pitched on the pummelled edge of a battlefield decorated with moaning, *so beloved*, blood-soaked men. Gone silent.

vi

I *will* be careful, Stranger.

Not to touch your hand. Your freckles, their light dusting
across your whole face! How they pool just under your brown eyes

as if a gathering.

These days I wish I could cross over.

III. Xenos: From the Posthumous Diaries of the Door

"Mother was a Tree. And Father, a Saw.
The things he saw! *What is a door …*
said Father. Said Mother:
A door is born to Adore or Abhor.

I am to admit Gusts and/or Guests.
I admit nothing! *When a Guest*
dressed best from head to toe –
To me, Mother bestowed a bark scroll

scribbled with The Grand Narratives:
The Archive of Aspirations, The Book
of Benevolence, The Charter of Charitable
Checkerboards … Whereas Father

bequeathed such binary thinking. Then,
a difference: sweaty violets,
the parlour inconsolable. Keep out!
But then you show up wearing such bright bags!

On either side
of me, a Stranger or a Stranger.
Past the Doorman."

IV. Sister Xenia in the Museum

i

All afternoon, she waits
for the outer doors to close
to the public so she can go back to her dancing.

She used to practise
on tippytoes, in lingerie shop windows,
butter knives.

You are obscene,
her little sister would hiss.
That's right, obscene. It just means offstage!
she'd snap back.

Her favourite thing
is to play among dioramas.
She is a conductor. *No,*
I am an ambassador.
She loves to fuck up his work.

ii

In the studio.
The taxidermized shapes become.
My half-formed daughters, the taxidermist calls them.

She likes to imagine
his waxen brow,
the taxidermist's furred fore-lip –
how it would crinkle, wrinkle and shrivel up
if he caught her as she lays her palm
cool upon their tanned skins.

Then to powder them with the pads
of her fingertips.

The mannequins perform
female nudity.

As positioned,
meticulously measured
forms of wood, wool, polyurethane
and wire, each, the spitting image of.
First, I mount them,
he says.
Stenches
of formaldehyde, soda ash
and glue punch air.
He will pull real skins over the forms,
then install glass eyes: bright,
specular, stuck fast in sockets.
Then the clay cheekbones.
His initials carved into the soft pads of our feet.
Then I will finish them.

When the creator leaves for the night:
The Chorus.

Daughters-in-waiting
for a man to say when our lives
will look realistically real.

It happens slowly.
Touch, a form of attention.

The seeking shape of maize.
Its horn oblong, or tusklets violetting
each flesh bead rises ochre nests to purpling.
The ceramic eyes of quiet daughters.

The face
considers
the painting:
Still Life of Vegetables.

In tin cans' oneiric ditches,
vegetal broths froth and bubble
up amber on the workbench
made from the crotch
of a pine tree.

Grace. The hospital.
Unborn shape of herself.
Her name means two things.

One of the things is the word for
the gift given to a guest
or stranger, which
being received makes them
no longer a stranger.

She is also what happens
when she whispers, *Tonight.*
She whispers it.

Unlike all cloistered others.
Her speech pressed the magenta blush
to stain crimson, blotching the face
of the Mayor's son.

Letter Y:
<u>Yet</u>

Already born, her antlers but small nubs. Like erasers. *"Not yet,"* say the High Chins.

Dust squalls encircle her minuscule frame. Adrift, her gentle confetti rehearses slowness.

"Her mother?" "A seesaw." "Check."

"Her father?" "A fountain pen who leaked at both ends." "Check."

It is Almost Time, again. The Between-Girls bandage her scraped knee

with the russet prom dress of a caterpillar. The One with the Magnificent Lipstick
and "That Red Pen!" adds a line in the Inventory.

Inventory, Inventory of Unfinished Things.

"And: *yet*." When they leave, she underlines it twice.

She rests her chin at the edge of the bottom stair ledge, a ridge. The carpet,

a vista. She will memorize this. Within it one hundred miniature elk create a
single shape as they flee.

Letter Z:
Cryptozoology Abecedarium –
The Garden of Intelligence, or, The Fitting Room

The letters of the alphabet are contemporaries of death.

EDMOND JABÈS, *The Book of Questions: Vol. II*, Trans. Rosmarie Waldrop

Agoraphobic, an Astronomer asks and asks, aspires "to archive Alterity,

But bravely" the Baker of Brutalities berates recipes, rings up the Biology Mistress or, the

Cat creeps, a Collector of Chaos and Camp, consults carnage, concupiscent Cartographer of Collapse:

"Divination!" – to Defer! as you must, Doctor Deficit, in your desire for the Duchess of Mudflaps,

Employed as Éditrice for the Eulogy of Elegy, eminently underqualified, emphatically "Exempt

From Feigning," the Foreign Minister of Fake Fruit fawns over forgeries, fathoms ekphrasis, for,

Grandpa Gustav Gravitas gorges, gurgles from his gelatin giblet: "Gone! Gone. Gone, are ..."

Her hands hold the box with the girl on the box holding a box with the girl on the box, "*Here,   ?*"

In the midst of Interpreters of Interstice, interpellative, from the Intercom, something informed I that:

"*Je est un autre!*" jokes the best jester who juggles jingles and jackknives,

Knowing that Killing Floors, kaleidoscopic, cannot keep kitchen maids kindly for

Long, on a loop, Lottie's Lollipop Lottery, carnivalesque, can it liberate Labourers? or the Little

Matchmaker in the Museum of Margins mixing batter with moons and Matchgirls in it;

Needless to say, nonce never negates, names near-extinct *Once More Than Never*, nearly

Orphans! organize the drawer of ostracized forks in which she will sleep operatic,

Preparing, the Piano Tuner of Earthquakes plots protocols of paradox in his pair of Docs with

Queen Eugene! so busy in his quest to question the quagmire of the Query, not quite

Rhyming, Rita refutes representation, rehearses, her backward-rearing hearse, remembers:

Said the Sequined Non Sequitur, "O, my spectacle!" insurgent Spinster, since

The tablecloth is a napkin for a giant troll; ice cubes made from tap water teem, once were paternal pterodactyl tears

"Unutterable, Buttercup!" utters an Usher, hirsute and unabashed as *Une Tasse en Fourrure*, unless –

Vexing, Ventriloquists invoke violence in villages: "Villainy among Violet Sellers, in vanitas!"
In velvet,

We weathered Winter; waded for the word "water" in the Word Well; weathered Want, and When

Extremist, the Empress of Empathy endures elephantine emptiness as she awaits, ever, only,
for exactly:

You – yourself! yelling away at Yellow Yesterdays with your yardstick *"Yak, yak, yak!"* – yes! your

Zookeeper corrals zirconia zebras who go zipping by, "To the Fitting Room! *For once, can't we keep zigzags organized!"*

Letter A:
Apostrophe Essay
Addendum: on the Letter A

...

I was staring in a frame:
inside itself, its platform was floating,

leaning against infinity.
Space framed by space

abiding, I thought, "attention is
already patience." Is it

perhaps a ladder?" Or a crane,
an altar or the hammered stand

or stall: that place for the absent
doll, arranged upon a plank.

Could her face and arms
be poseable? Her gasp the sound

of matter rasping still. Yet expanding,
incantatory from within

her miniature wardrobe. Fragile.
is her naked glance at the safest,

and inaudible, audience.
Despite their binoculars, she's still

unwatched. Not yet named,
nor taken. She aches rare and solitary.

She gapes at without. And is akin

to that wounding

absence that must create
its own company –

but can it. Can it,
without capture, usher.

Usher in, from its station
or portal,

some watching. *Yours?*
"Which changes her." Somewhat

like abyss: a blank page, a parental
space, ancient,

near melancholy,
intimate that sad fantastic pause,

or gash, wherein commandments
arrive, on the back of a postage stamp.

(We cannot know the true name
of her patron.) "Not a thing

is hers."
From the vantage of a balcony, or

an opera box. I could watch
the actors, I thought: "What trauma!

A shape was arranging,
or was it learning"

from the transcript of Within,

where one can only ever ask:

"Am I that That?" The caretaker:
anatomy, galactic lacking, company

that practises detachment
or separation,

that the Handbook states
 is required "to enable relation,

or affection." At eight o'clock,
the man arrives underdressed and begins to imitate

the antique cake stand
of that aging Baroness who stands

aslant,
at her own lawn sale –

(where she sells thumbtacks, a mid-war furnace. Syntax.
Worn gold chains that "Still work." A chipped flask.

Who made this!")
Her monogrammed handkerchief, laid out, and if

she catches you admiring it she will say,
delicately, as you retract your hand,

"Here – take it" – the man disappears,
yet is still here. He is the space

that transforms thread to lace.
As I reach for even just

the warped hem of his musty jacket –

I am still safe – from the clang

of malice, mistakes. Machinations of self-

interest, violence.
From this vantage, am I still undamaged –

be it, "Just an accident," or *"Which is worse?"* deliberate –
within an elevator made of glass.

Nevertheless, what might become.
If I said *"But can we ..."* Until then,

the vacant lots between you and I
may gestate meaning antimatter, and

resemblance: a lattice is "the distance between us
that enables craving."

(And address.) But can it not just alter –
as domination – rather, can it

(must it) transform (every her
up on her swing-less porcelain swing). And not yet –

claim her Alterity as in otherness –
that nostalgic drawing of that hat

which in the dream someone wore
to the wake as if apart and within

an opening which the yielding mind
admits itself to be

more rooms, within and without And

yet conjoining, several spectacles

of how it is that You, comprise me
among many (me) of which I am but one.

FIN.

✦ Poems: Biographies ✦

Letter C: "'Chloe liked Olivia.' by Mary Carmichael and, or, Virginia Woolf"

When a room is a laboratory. How Virginia laboured. Virginia published
A Room of One's Own in 1929.

Within its rooms, Virginia spoke of Mary Carmichael in the fifth chapter.
Mary was the author of a book entitled *Life's Adventure*. Virginia admired
how Mary wrote on unorthodox topics and within unorthodox styles, in terms
of the forms of intelligence that were considered acceptable, possible, for
women. Virginia was astonished to read Mary's statement:
"Chloe liked Olivia."

"Chloe liked Olivia" was a revolutionary utterance to Virginia. In that, therein,
Mary imagined the possibility of *other* relations among women: an ethos of
admiration, and deliberate, rather than enforced, care; above all, relationality
unmediated by patriarchs. In a room that is a laboratory, in order. In order to
imagine this, Virginia invented it. Virginia invented both Mary and Mary's book.
She had had to invent new rooms for them. And disorderly in language to make
them imaginable.

Virginia made room. It is rumoured that the name Mary Carmichael is derived
from a sixteenth-century Scottish ballad, among the Child Ballads that so often
narrated tales revolving around plots of violence against women. From Ballad
173, the Fower Maries, a tale based, possibly, on the four unwed ladies-in-
waiting to Mary, Queen of Scots. One Mary among them was executed for
infanticide and/or for having an affair with the King that had produced the threat
of an illegitimate heir.

Within the laboratory of Virginia's language, this vill*a*inelle was born. From
phrases within its room named Chapter Five. In which Virginia imagined that
Mary could imagine that "Chloe liked Olivia" so that we could imagine that.
I have maintained the syntax of Virginia's original phrases and, as indicated by
the use of parentheses and periods, I have "broken" her "sequence" and
"sentence(s)." Because I like her.

Letter E: The Education of Little Miss Muffet

But she must have had thoughts while she sat on her tuffet.
The "Little Miss Muffet" nursery rhyme may have been inspired by the real-life
girl named Patience Mouffet.

Patience was the stepdaughter of Dr. Thomas Mouffet (1553–1604),
the first British scientist to catalogue insects.
Historians continue to debate the nursery rhyme's origins.
Her own story remains unrecorded therein.
Author of *The Theater of Insects; or, Lesser Living Creatures*, Dr. Mouffet is
said to have fed Patience spiders
as a medical treatment. None have said whether Patience wanted them inside her.
During this time, many medical practitioners believed that the ingestion
of spiders could cure a wide variety of ailments in question.
Spiders were eaten live, of course. They were also worn as pendants or chokers,
and integrated into common recipes, by choice or by force.

In her 1914 article "How It Feels to Be Forcibly Fed," Djuna Barnes wrote:
"It was the most concentrated moment of my life." She published this article
after willingly submitting herself to be force-fed by doctors, in her solidarity
with contemporary hunger-striking female suffragettes who were being
restrained, and then, to this practice, subjected.

Thinking himself an expert on the subject, Hippocrates wrote of the Womb,
Hystera. Considering the womb migratory, Hippocrates declared it bad, and sad.
Ancient Egyptians, too, believed it to wander the halls of the Female Body,
causing ailments with symptoms ranging from the very fluctuation of emotions,
depression, innumerable symptoms now identified as PTSD and derangements
such as *the fondness for writing*: all of which were once considered forms of
"hysteria."

To induce fondness for writing and elocution,
British hornbooks were small, tablets used as primers for educating children
as early as 1326, up to the late eighteenth century, in Britain.
Letters of the alphabet and the Lord's Prayer were fondly written

onto a small frame from which extended a handle. The tablet was covered
with parchment much like butcher paper. Sometimes made of gingerbread,
hornbooks doubled in function:
as punitive paddle for imprecise recitations,
and as edible reward upon successful elocution.

Dorothea Tanning, a Surrealist-affiliated artist, painted wild mindscapes of the
lives of girls and women. She once described her childhood home as the place
"where nothing happens but the wallpaper."
But she must have had thoughts while she sat.

I do not speculate regarding the actual lives of the historic famille Mouffet.
Rather, I offer a poetic imaginary, in exploration of the cultural history
within which this ubiquitous nursery
rhyme was born. As per accounts of the lives of women and girls considered
to be legal "property,"
I write this for that imaginary, nameless girl whom everyone called silly
for having shrieked, perhaps quite thoughtfully,
from that tuffet.

Letter G: The Gift

How she rendered.
Etymologically, from the Latin, "Reddere" –
That the "red" is *to return,*

To surrender. And the given,
From "dere": *to give.* Then further
And further, and bending, she rendered

In the fourteenth century, the term for that: *to reduce fats,*
To transform carcasses and waste into oils for fertilizer, and also,
To turn into tallow for soap. Then shifting, or perhaps cleansed

Or mended, in the 1400s, extended, the term:
To return payment, a legal term. And shifting interminably, in the 1580s,
To render, *is to alter by violence*. Yet, lent, alternately,
And signifies art; so again she renders, contending: to *represent, to perform,*
Interpretation, as in. Drawing, literature, illustration.
To render is to pass down without ending; *through which*
To transform. A form.

Letter H: Halfpenny Opera – *The Adventures of Two Pincushion Dolls*; *Les Demimondaines, Poem II*

Once Upon a Time, There Was a Woman Who Spins

flax in ancient Egypt, and elsewhere also cotton, silk and wool. Manual textile work was considered domestic and therefore almost exclusively the work of women. In the 1300s, women who spun thread were typically poor and used spinning wheels, while wealthier thread and fabric workers could afford to use a loom. As a poorly paid profession, the art of spinning nevertheless enabled some women to earn a modicum of financial self-sufficiency, should she find herself, for example, unmarried or widowed.

Unmarried women's self-sufficiency, combined with the very fact of their being unwed, was frequently met with resentment. In the 1700s, "spinster" was a legal term for a profession, however it became a derisive term for the identity of an unmarried woman who, presumably, was deservedly also impoverished. The derogatory use of the term "spinster" inferred that the unwed spinning woman must be undesirable, unlikely to marry due to her lack of beauty, or to disability or aging.

Famous literary spinsters include Charles Dickens's Miss Havisham (who was in her thirties) and the beguiling poet Stevie Smith. Historic portrayals of spinsters frequently ascribed witchlike (pagan and/or magical), asexual, non-Christian and sexually subversive attributes. This was most likely due to spinsters' gender transgressions, which were initially economic, and also, on behalf of spinsters' symbolic power to model alternate relationalities, for example, relations other than heteronormative monogamous marriage and father-centred bloodline families. In the 1200s, versions of the spinning wheel with increased technologies that could have made the profession more widely accessible were briefly banned in France and termed "The Devil's Work."

Once Upon a Time She Was a Pincushion

Pincushion Dolls or Half-Dolls were popular from the late 1800s to the 1930s in France, Germany/Bavaria, England, Japan and the US. Some were hand-painted, some mass-produced. Some had just porcelain heads, or a head and a bust; some had porcelain arms, and in rarer cases, bisque legs were also attached to the pincushion section with glue, making these the most costly. None possessed a porcelain torso;

rather, this separate portion of the half-doll was stuffed with some form of cloth. Skirt- or crinoline-shaped, and designed to hold pins, her torso was sometimes empty, a covered space within which to "camouflage" everyday objects – *"anything that needed to be covered up"* (teapots, whisks, powder boxes). Some have said that half-dolls, of hybrid construction, were, therefore, neither "real" dolls, nor "authentic" pincushions. The most famous Victorian pincushion resided in the children's book *Adventures of a Pincushion: Designed Chiefly for the Use of Young Ladies* (1780/1783), written by British children's author Mary Ann Kilner. She originally published under the pseudonym S.S. (which stood for her home, Spital Square) so that readers could think her works were written by a man.

The phrase "spouting the nonsense of swans" is quoted from Lisa Robertson's *XEclogue* (New Star Books, 1999), with generous permission from the author.

Once Upon a Time, "A Cage! A Crinoline!"

The crinoline was invented in 1856 by R.C. Milliet, who patented this metal cage in Paris, designed so as to enhance a woman's silhouette according to an imagined form of the female body. Its purpose was to shape her. The cage crinoline created the underlying illusion of the tiniest waist possible. It outdid earlier hooped skirts such as the sixteenth- and seventeenth-century farthingales and the eighteenth-century panniers, all of which enabled her skirts to so very vastly *poof!* It was introduced to England by France's Empress Eugénie in the late 1850s and was at the peak of fashion a fad that swept across England and its colonies (including the United States) and Europe in the 1860s until the late 1870s when it was replaced by smaller crinolettes and lesser bustles.

Constructed of horsehair ("crin") and fabrics such as cotton, and then encased in whalebone or steel, the crinoline was an invention that enflamed much contention. Some praised it for allowing women greater mobility than earlier restrictive corsets, which could now be forgotten, while others debated its potential immorality. Many denounced it. In an era in which women who could not afford to feed their babies sometimes sought forbidden abortions, many claimed (albeit an entirely nonsensical argument) that it could be misused to hide forbidden pregnancy. At the time, cartoons in multiple dailies saw male cartoonists making a mockery – all these enlarged women suddenly taking up forbidden public space! Many decided that as a vehicle capable of enlarging female agency, the crinoline would result in imperilling "a woman's proper reputation, and safety."

Initially, that mention of safety did not mean actual concern for crinoline-wearing women; rather, it signified worry that their (previously less mobilized) reputations remain intact, without the faintest hint of wandering, independence or rebellion. At the outset, none predicted how many women would deploy the crinoline for smuggling, nor how many women would meet their deaths by it.

Reports of Under-Crinoline-Smuggling as linked to theft and attempts to elude restrictive immigration rules included the hiding of, on one particular occasion, no fewer than twelve partridges. And other times also: turkeys, rabbits, one man hid his sizable leg of mutton, others hid tobacco, tea and gin. One woman on a train hid a full-grown man who had no ticket. It was also reported that women could transport medicines to soldiers on the front lines under crinolines just as some had succeeded in doing by hiding medicines in the bodies of dolls.

Popularized by women across most classes, the crinoline proved too absurdly constricting for the poorest of working women. However, women from upper and middle classes, as well as ladies' maids and factory girls, also took to it.

The crinoline took the lives of women by the thousands. Falls and catching on carriage doors and carriage wheels became common, fatal accidents. In an era of candles and fireplaces, the most common death-by-crinoline was the being-set-aflame of women who could neither move swiftly, nor escape from within its metal cage. As it happened, popular crinoline fabrics such as tulle and gauze were highly flammable, and further, any flame-retardant fabrics were prohibitively costly. Moreover, these huge swaths of fabric were cleaned by hand, often sprayed with extremely flammable cleaning solutions, for example, kerosene, which is petroleum-based. The great space under the crinoline only accelerated the infernos. Women were described as having literally "burst into flame."

Among the famous, Oscar Wilde's two half-sisters, Emily and Mary, died by crinoline-fire; one had waltzed near a fireplace, caught fire, and then her sister tried to save her. Both were consumed in flames. And Fanny, wife to poet Henry Wadsworth Longfellow, also died in this way while she was heating wax close to a packet that contained a lock of her child Edie's snipped curls. Later, Oscar helped campaign with his friend Henrietta Vaughan Stannard, founder of the Anti-Crinoline League, for the more "rational dress" for women. This tragic event had remained somewhat hushed (Oscar's half-sisters improperly named on the coroner's certificate to preserve his father's reputation, in that they had been illegitimate); nevertheless, for twenty years to follow, a mysterious woman clad in black visited their quiet graves. While lesser known (since ballerinas were considered at the time to be of little value, and barely a step above what they called "the common prostitute"), ballerinas had been going up in flames for decades all over the world (for example in France, England, the US, Brazil and Italy). In that same year in which Fanny was killed by crinoline fire so was the famous ballerina Marie Taglioni (1832).

Victorian author Charles Dickens, who created the character Dolly Varden, also ended his popular novel *Great Expectations* with a dress fire. The dress of the spinster, Miss Havisham, burst into flames. Some have suggested this connoted her brittleness, blamed for never having removed her wedding dress after being defrauded at the altar.

Upon catching fire, Miss Havisham asked for forgiveness. All she had ever hoped for was to keep another woman, Estella, safe from harm at the hands of men. (Perhaps also for a wee bit of revenge.) She hoped to protect Estella with her only weapon – a whole lot of money, or failing that, Miss Havisham hoped they could rely on the failsafe protection of Estella's beauty.

Letter I: Intermission, The Image; Phenakistoscope Poem

Invented in 1832, the Phenakistoscope was lent its name from the Greek "phenakizein":

"Phenakistes" meant "deceiving" or "cheating," "an imposter"
+ "skopos" was the "one who watches,"

and/or (interestingly) "skopos," also: as the "object of attention"
watched by the watcher.

A Phenakistoscope is held among other artifacts in the Musée Patamécanique, Rhode Island, a private museum. Part automaton theatre, part cabinet of curiosities, its collection is greatly inspired by legacies of Dada, Surrealism and the 'Pataphysics of Alfred Jarry. It also contains a machine for capturing the dreams of bumblebees!

An optical toy and early animation device, such toys combined popular scientific discoveries with the act of looking itself; Victorian viewing became a species of recreation. During this time, zoos, the circus and sideshows, and displays of life-sized dioramas in auditoriums were also in fashion The phenakistoscope was a precursor of film technology. It creates the illusion of a suite of identical repeated images in motion, following one another around in a continuous circle of imposter and her sisters all watching watched watchers.

Letter L: Line Dance

Both choliambic and iambic metres (or rhythms) have been compared with "limping." However, the earliest mythological engagements with Iambe were in fact magical: let us recall the story that the deity Iambe assuaged Demeter – who was in the throes of grieving her abducted daughter Persephone – by embodying some transformative, sublime and secret words. In her body of iambic metre.

Choliambic verse is sometimes called "scazon," or "lame iambic" because it brings the reader down on the "wrong foot" by reversing the stresses of the last few beats. It was originally pioneered by the Greek lyric poet Hipponax, who wrote "lame trochaics" as well as "lame iambics," iambic metre ending with a trochee or, more often, a spondee.

Iambic metre was imported to English verse from Italian/Greco-Roman origins and is often, and perhaps more aptly, beautifully, compared to the most elemental music: that of the human heartbeat.

Letter P: Polly Pollen

From dust; from flour; from grounded seed –
The etymological origins of the word "pollen";
That singular noun for that condition. Of multiplicity,
Are inherited, internationally, and many
Plants grow "perfect" flowers. Hermaphroditic, this art
Of possessing both male (androecium) and female
(Gynoecium) reproductive parts. And studies
By way of conversations with young children
Demonstrate that many exhibit great curiosity, and anxiety
Regarding "the rules" of gender – what a "boy" or a "girl"
Or a "her" or a "him" – and what else
Can our bodies engender. This poem plays
With errors and/or resistances against conventional grammar
(Which is to say the world) by quoting children's actual early linguistic
Inventions. Their fluid terminologies, about gender and possibility,

Are ample and borrowed (for example, "her-her," "him-her")
From CHILDES research transcriptions (studies
Of Infant/child language acquisition).

Letter Q: "One Final Touch-Up Before the Coronation ..."; Queen Bee Poem

In the beginning, a Beehive. In which the daughters gathered ...

Medieval Christian nuns in Europe were sometimes charged with the task to gather for the making of beeswax flowers for altars, effigies and ceremonies.

Later, in the 1730s and '40s, Martha Gazeley, a British wax artist, offered colonials and nuns instruction as titled, "Wax Work, Nuns' Work for Young Gentlewomen." As it happens, many British queens were obsessed, especially Queen Victoria, both with the display of flowers made of wax, and with their possession.

(Poem II: *Work Song: Punk Rock Chorus Line* – "Wax Work, Nuns' Work for Young Gentlewomen.")

The term "moat of pearl" is derived from "Did the Harebell loose her girdle," one of Emily Dickinson's many poems about bees, albeit about them only partially.

(Poem III: The Sex Lives of Queens.)

The question "Who is responsible for the suffering of your mother?" is borrowed from Bhanu Kapil's *The Vertical Interrogation of Strangers* (Kelsey Street Press, 2001), an artistic rendering gathered from interviews with women of East Indian descent, in which the women were asked a series of twelve elemental questions about their lives, with her kind permission.

(Poem VI: Interview with the Daughters: *Chorus.*)

The phrase "the man in white smiles, bare-handed" is derived from one of Sylvia Plath's bee poems "Stings."

(Poem VII: Mausoleum Lullaby: In Memoriam for My Death.)

Stephen Buchmann is thanked for his research on the "knowing" held by bees, who, as it happens, learn in their sleep, recognize human faces that have caused them harm

and may even dream.

Letter S: The Story of the Striped Cravat and the Striped Uniform

The Necktie: A Biography

Many attribute its ubiquity to Louis VIII, who, during the Thirty Years War (in 1618, a war ostensibly invested in the freedom of religion, yet tied up with concerns economic) espied and admired Croatian mercenary soldiers who wore the kravata (the cloth of red) at their throats, either to wipe up blood or sweat, or to be visible to their beloved women who watched from the hills while they battled in valleys. This went on to become mandated as the Croatian military uniform, made from either coarse cloth or silk ("svila"). Louis VIII was so enchanted by the sight of it that he ordered all males at Royal Gatherings to wear it.

The cravat went on to become a sign of elegance and culture in France, in fact, a signifier of power and privilege. Seeing this, King Charles II then adopted it in English court. The Windsor knot was popularized by the Duke of Windsor in the 1930s. Before and after this, ever-shifting fads arose – imposed, interpellated or chosen – that established which knots, fabric, sizes and arrangements were au courant, and just how (on earth) to tie it. Memorably, Winston Churchill refused and refastened it by adopting the bow tie, which, some suggest, was to signify his humble origins.

Alternately, Fashion Historians also purport that this masculine habit originated with the Chinese emperor Quin Shih Huang, who was buried with terracotta warriors with knotted swaths at their necks in 210 BCE. After that, Roman emperor Traianus (Trajan) had a column built that depicted valiant Roman soldiers with handsome neckcloths.

All origin stories engage the significance of the man's necktie as a fashion accessory that spake "Empire …" from about a man's throat.

Letter T: Part Two – Trading Beauty Secrets with the Dead: The Dolly Varden Esssay

Part One: References to Rainer Maria Rilke's reactions are derived from his 1914 essay "Puppen. Zu den Wachs-Puppen von Lotte Pritzel," translated by Idris Parry as "Dolls: On the Wax Dolls of Lotte Pritzel," in *On Dolls*, edited by Kenneth Gross (New York: New York Review of Books, 2023).

Part One: Rainer Maria Rilke's "Duino Elegies" was translated by Stephen Mitchell.

Part Two: Egyptian and Greek names in this section are derived from Sophie Kambitsis, "Une nouvelle tablette magique d'Égypte. Musée du Louvre, inv. E 27145 – IIIe/IVe siècle," *Bulletin de l'Institut français d'archéologie orientale* 76 (1976): 213–23.

Part Two: Charles Baudelaire's seminal essay "The Philosophy of Toys" (1853) was translated by Jonathan Mayne.

Part Five: "God Is Man's Doll, You Ass!" is derived from Stevie Smith's poem "Was He Married?" in which the narrator claims that Man makes up such a doll "on purpose."

Letter X: Xenos – Excerpts from *The Handbook: How to Play with Children from Another Species*

The ancient Greek word "xenos" was born in Homeric times, meaning "guest-friend":

"an elite social peer from somewhere else with whom you have reciprocal inherited hospitality obligations" (Kemezis). Then, at some point in the seventh or sixth century BCE, vertical bonds within city states became more important and the word's meaning broadened, to signify any foreign or alien person.

Interestingly, the word "hostis" also went through a kindred transformation, signifying, early on, something akin to "guest," and eventually becoming a standard word for "enemy," in written Latin.

My thanks to Professor Adam Kemezis, a Greek historian at the University of Alberta who specializes in the historiography of the Roman Empire, for assisting me to better understand the word's life history.

In her profound meditations on relationality Lyn Hejinian wrote:

> Poetry, at this time, I believe, has the capacity and perhaps the obligation to enter those specific zones know as borders, since borders are by definition addressed to foreignness, and in a complex sense, best captured in another Greek word, *xenos*. It, too, means 'stranger' or 'foreigner' ... The *xenos* figure is one of contradiction and confluence. ...
>
> ... Every encounter produces, even if for only the flash of an instant, a *xenia* – the occurrence of coexistence which is also an occurrence of strangeness and foreignness. ("Barbarism")

Let us please not forget her sister-word "xenia":

"Xenia" is a magical word. It denotes the effect that (foreign) pollen has on fruits and seeds, a spectacular, unimagined and transformative *collaboration*. In addition, "xenia" was a formulation for Greek "hospitality" with three rules: the Respect from Host to Guest, the Respect from Guest to Host and the Parting Gift from Guest to Host. Ancient Greek relations of hospitality were not identical to unconditional reciprocity. Greco-Roman hospitality was limited to confines of class, gender, nationality and, of course, species.

Letter Z: Cryptozoology Abecedarium – The Garden of Intelligence, or, The Fitting Room

Cryptozoology comprises the study of, and search for, *real and imagined* beings and beasts.

The etymological roots of the word "zoo" are imported from the ancient Greek word "zōion," meaning "living being." Zoological gardens began as royal playthings. An emperor in China in the twelfth-century BCE is said to have assembled a "garden of intelligence" with beasts imported for his collection. The abbreviation "zoo" was first used at the London Zoological Gardens, which was opened for scientific study in 1828 and to the public in 1847. In this cryptozoology, *Une Tasse en Fourrure*, also known as *Le Déjeuner en Fourrure* (translated variously as *A Teacup in Fur*, *The Luncheon in Fur* or *Fur Breakfast*) is the name of a sculpture/assemblage created by Surrealist artist Meret Oppenheim consisting of a fur-covered teacup, saucer and spoon (1936). She may have invented it as a dare, while chatting at a luncheon.

The Piano Tuner of Earthquakes is the name of a post-Surrealist stop-motion animated film by the Brothers Quay (2005).

This Biology Mistress (not to mention, the talking Cat) is imported with permission from Mary Jo Bang's poem "Silence Always Happens Suddenly"; Mary Jo reports that that Mistress was imported from a 1950s' British "girl's guide" series that someone gave her as a gift; the story is called "Mystery at Manor Close."

❦ Dedications and Acknowledgements ❦

Letter D: Debtor's Cabaret, Libretto for the Puppet Show;
Les Demimondaines, Poem I
This demi-play nods to *The Other Poems* by Paul Legault. My thanks for his
blessing to create a neighbourly retort to his beguiling sonnets.
Also, the ghost of Edward Gorey must surely walk these checkerboard floors.

Letter F: Folktale
Observing the noteworthy dearth of female "giants" within canonical Western
literature, my nod to Susan Stewart's studies of gigantism – as primarily
masculinist in Western culture, and by extension, when feminized: deemed
monstrous.

This poem is indebted to Michael Tavel Clarke's scholarly explorations of size
and the human body (*These Days of Large Things: The Culture of Size in
America, 1865–1930*), in particular, his nuanced study of anxieties regarding
gender and body size invoked by the film *Attack of the 50 Foot Woman* (1958).

Letter G: The Gift
Julie Joosten, for the gift of your mind and friendship.

This poem originally cherished Grandmother Clock as an "Old Woman," my
ongoing attempt to re-visibilize and celebrate the inestimable significance of
women as we age. With characteristic brilliance, in an earlier editorial session
Mary Jo Bang reminded me:

"And I don't like the idea of making this about 'Old' women . . . 'Old Women' is
also a patriarchal concept. Women are Women, regardless of their ages."

What brilliance.

Letter H: Halfpenny Opera – *The Adventures of Two Pincushion Dolls*;
Les Demimondaines, Poem II
For Lisa Robertson and the Hag.
The rhinestones are for Shooshi (played by Braden Welsh in *Tomato Girl* written
by Jacquelin Walters, 2024).

Letter L: Line Dance
For poet, performer and disabilities activist Brandon Wint.

Letter N: The Cameo Essay – Towards a Poetics of Nonsense
Thank you to Michèle Cohen of Black Swan Antiques (1991–2023) Edmonton,
for sharing her hard-won expertise, for helping that tiny cameo from Bavaria find
her way to me, and for friendship.

Research pertaining to the life of Marie Antoinette is derived from the
scholarship of Judith Thurman. Judith reports that Queen Marie is said to have
once said to her mother that her persecutions seemed to be the consequence of
the choice: "to be myself."

This poem extends gratitude to the work and mentorship of Don McKay, in
particular his brilliant poem "Fates Worse Than Death."

Letter P: Polly Pollen
For Empathy Scuttersgill Moure.

Letter R: Requiem for Our Hunting Fathers
For Jim (James) Ellis, scholar of Queer, Black and Experimental Film, who
introduced me to Wilfred Owen's poetics, most importantly to Owen's queering
of rhyme, "pararhyme." In his significant essay "Strange Meeting: Wilfred
Owen, Benjamin Britten, Derek Jarman, and the *War Requiem*" Jim explores the
counter-hegemonic works of these three artists. He writes: "To oppose the male

body to the nationalist ideologies sacrificing it is not to retreat from politics but to enter them at a more profound level. To privilege the body in this way is to begin to move toward a new form of sociality, one not based on a traumatic relation to difference" (284).

Letter S: The Story of the Striped Cravat and the Striped Uniform

Michael A. Bucknor's essay "Austin Clarke's 'Saga Boys': Black Aesthetics as Epistemology?" continues to remind me of the expansive significations of the "sartorial": its epistemological depths, and as a culturally specific – tactical and artful – vehicle for resistance.

Letter T: Part One – "(Never) The Time for Beauty";
Les Demimondaines, Poem III

For the work of Vivek Shraya. In particular, her illuminating explorations of misogyny as a primary foundation of homophobia.

Letter T: Part Two – Trading Beauty Secrets with the Dead:
The Dolly Varden Esssay

I am indebted to the work and support of the following scholars:

Laura Severin, whose recuperative scholarship on the writing *and* artwork of Stevie Smith honours Stevie by taking her *playful* drawings *"seriously"*;

Julie Sims Steward, whose incisive scholarship on the oeuvre of Stevie Smith, including Stevie's brilliant engagement with millinery, arrived at just the right time;

Rebecca N. Mitchell, for studies of the Dolly Varden dress fad and its related cultural history;

Steve Birks, for sharing research on the historic British bone china/porcelain factories, and on working conditions for the women and girls who painted in the porcelain/ceramics industry in the 1920s;

Kathryn Hughes, for scholarship pertaining to Victorian "domestication" of factories;

Sara Ayres, for incisive scholarship on the much-neglected artist Lotte Pritzel whose work is still too rarely discussed in detail (yet!) in English;

The unnamed staff at the Louvre Museum who tirelessly assisted me to locate "The Louvre Doll" and related photographic and archaeological documentation;

Sophie Kambitsis and Pierre du Bourguet for their important scholarship on the Louvre Doll (including photographs, inventories and translations). Sophie, translations and paraphrases from French to English herein, of the inscribed tablet, are mine. I did my best.

Ute-Brigitte Blunck, who generously advised regarding the full context of the German song "Die Lorelei."

Letter U: The Understudy; from *The Chronicles of Chloe and Olivia*; *Les Demimondaines, Poem V*

iii. Event Script for Rhinestones
This poem nods admiringly to Yoko Ono's conceptual "artist book" *Grapefruit* (1964) and its artworks of the imagination.

Letter V: Varorium, the Imperfect Villainelle
Les Demimondaines, Poem VI
Indebted to the work of Phyllis Wheatley, this is for Jackie Grieb, *still and always*.

Letter W: The Watchers; "*In the Aspic Academy ...*"
For Candace E. Oliver CEO, "Candy," Chief Epicurean Officer.

Letter X: Xenos – Excerpts from *The Handbook: How to Play with Children from Another Species*

For Lyn Hejinian, who has just departed.

Therein, **The Xebec Boats** is for Paul Harris, 1946–2020.

Letter Z: Cryptozoology Abecedarium – The Garden of Intelligence, or, The Fitting Room

Daniil Kharms and Bruno Schulz, respectively: *For the tumbling women!* *For the mobs of saucepans!*

✺ **Confetti** ✺

Words cannot.

My gratitude to *the Language Nurses*:
Amanda White, Therese Lloyd, Mary Jo Bang, Julie Joosten, Becky Blake, Suzette Mayr.

And to *the Rhyming Women*,
without whom this book and her author simply would not.

I am indebted to the following thinkers:

Jack Zipes, for his studies of folk and fairy tales as allegorizations of difference, and as fantasies of radical change to public power structures.

Victor Turner, for his explorations of the ethos of play as a subversive, performative force.

Susan Stewart, for her studies of nonsense as an elemental force, and as a process.

Dennis Lee, for nonsense verses, and for the provocation:

> I hope it's clear by now that I don't romanticize children ...
>   What I was thinking is this ... 'For shame! Thought control! Mother Goose is an imperialist conspiracy!'" ("Roots and Play").

John Borrows, for patient guidance on the subject of Two Row Wampum.

Reuben Quinn, whose teachings and conversations about Cree ways of knowing have been a gift.

The late Canadian psychoanalyst M.D. Faber, who observed that infants and children begin to engage in rhyme during the exact stage of identity development in which their forming selves negotiate "individuation" from the mother or caretaker. He posited that rhyme is a linguistic *and* psychological structure that embodies the *life-long* paradoxical challenge to grapple with simultaneous conditions: difference *and* resemblance, or attachment *and* separation.

The late Katherine Nelson is thanked for her illuminating studies of "crib narratives," and, by extension, the interpellative construction of the human self via the internalization of the speech of others.

The empathetic poetics of Selima Hill.

Meditations on lyric poetry and apostrophe herein are indebted to the thinking of Barbara Johnson, Claudia Rankine, Julie Joosten. And Jonathan Culler, for his generative claim that "such apostrophes may raise or be used to raise questions about who or what is the speaker and who or what the addressee, but in the first instance they are embarrassing: embarrassing both to the author and his (*sic*) readers."

Marshall Ward (1971–2023) for life-sustaining friendship. I cannot yet imagine my life, onwards, without the Gift of your Questions.

Please bow, or curtsy:

Thank you to the publishers who have given this work a home, in particular *filling Station* + Marc Lynch, and *EXILE* literary quarterly + the Callaghan families.

I am grateful for the creative research grants awarded by the Writers' Guild of Alberta, the Alberta Foundation for the Arts, the Edmonton Arts Council and the Canada Council for the Arts.

How you shimmer: Larissa Lai. Michael Tavel Clarke, Joanna Card, Cecily Devereux, Christine Wiesenthal and Eddy Kent.

Honoured to find a home with Buckrider Books imprint, Wolsak & Wynn Publishers once again. Confetti for Noelle Allen, Ashley Hisson, Jen Rawlinson. And to the risk-taking, original Buckrider himself, Paul Vermeersch: my unswerving appreciation.

Dana Holst, for her permission to grace the cover of this book with her sublime painting *In the Dark*.

Kilby Smith-McGregor for unimagined empathetic Design.

And for my students:

What you teach me. Thank you, Beasts.

About the Author

Erina Harris is a Canadian writer, educator and mentor. Her first book, *The Stag Head Spoke* (Buckrider Books, 2014), was shortlisted for the Canadian Authors Association Award for Poetry. A graduate and Fellow of the Iowa Writers' Workshop, her work has been published widely, translated and awarded multiple prizes and international residencies. She lives and teaches in Edmonton.